Spy Science

Other Titles of Interest by Jim Wiese

Roller Coaster Science

50 Wet, Wacky, Wild, Dizzy Experiments
about Things Kids Like Best

Rocket Science

50 Flying, Floating, Flipping, Spinning Gadgets
Kids Create Themselves

Detective Science

40 Crime-Solving, Case-Breaking, Crook-Catching
Activities for Kids

Spy Science

40 Secret-Sleuthing, Code-Cracking, Spy-Catching Activities for Kids

Jim Wiese

Illustrations by Ed Shems

JOSSEY-BASS
A Wiley Imprint
www.josseybass.com

Published by Jossey-Bass
A Wiley Imprint
989 Market Street, San Francisco, CA 94103-1741   www.josseybass.com

Published simultaneously in Canada.

Jossey-Bass books and products are available through most bookstores. To contact Jossey-Bass directly call our Customer Care Department within the U.S. at 800-956-7739, outside the U.S. at 317-572-3986, or fax 317-572-4002.

Jossey-Bass also publishes its books in a variety of electronic formats. Some content that appears in print may not be available in electronic books.

Library of Congress Cataloging-in-Publication Data

Wiese, Jim.
    Spy science : 40 secret-sleuthing, code-cracking, spy-catching
    activities for kids / Jim Wiese ; illustrations by Ed Shems.
        p. cm.
    Summary: Describes the skills, equipment, and techniques that spies use. Includes activities and experiments.
    Includes index.
    ISBN 0-471-14620-X (alk. paper)
    1. Espionage—Juvenile literature.   2. Intelligence service—Juvenile literature.
    [1. Espionage.   2. Intelligence service.   3. Experiments.]   I. Title.
    JF1525.I6W48   1996
    363.2'5931—dc20   96-7019

Printed in the United States of America
FIRST EDITION
PB Printing   SKY10030600_101921

For Barbara

My life is richer because I met you.

Acknowledgments

From my early days of watching the television show *The Man from U.N.C.L.E.* and reading books like Ian Fleming's James Bond series, I've always enjoyed slipping out of my mundane life into the exciting world of spies and secret agents. In researching this book, I drew first from my early interest in the gadgets that secret agents use. I remember making my first periscope when I was in third grade. More recently, the staff at Spy vs. Spy, The Spy Store in Vancouver were very helpful. They opened their store to me and showed me the newest available surveillance equipment and discussed ways that these items might become projects for the book.

As always, my special thanks go to Kate Bradford and Kara Raezer at John Wiley & Sons, Inc. The amount of support that they provided during the development of this book was incredible. They helped direct and shape my early proposal, and gave suggestions and edits all along the way. Jude Patterson's excellent copyediting also helped turn this into a finely crafted book of which I am proud. Thanks again!

Contents

Introduction

Spies and spying are fascinating. But real-life spying is danger-
ous work. Spies go on difficult missions to gather secret information, make contact with other spies, and pass on their secret
messages. To keep from getting caught—and to get the information they need—good spies have to learn the skills and techniques of the spy trade.

You may be surprised to learn that science often helps spies do
their work. Spies use all sorts of scientific and technical
devices to gather information. But the main tools they use are
their brains. Spies blend simple scientific knowledge with creative thinking to give them an edge.

This book will let you investigate the tricks of the spy trade,
build special spy equipment, and discover the secrets of how
spies use science to do their jobs.

How to Use This Book

Each chapter contains many exciting projects and experiments,
and every project has a list of materials you'll need and a
procedure to follow. Some of the projects have a section called
More Fun Stuff to Do that lets you try different variations on
the original activity. Another section called Spy Science in
Action shows you how the scientific principles you
learned doing the activity have been used in real life.
Words in **bold** type are defined in text and in the glossary
at the back of the book.

You'll be able to find most of the equipment you need for
the activities around the house and at your neighborhood
hardware, pharmacy, electronics, or grocery store. You
don't need expensive equipment to do the activities.
You need only an open mind that asks questions and
looks for answers. After all, the basis of any good
investigation is asking good questions and finding the
best answers.

How to Perform the Activities

- Read through the instructions once completely and collect all the equipment you'll need before you start the activity.

- Keep a notebook. Write down what you do in your project and what happens.

- Follow the instructions carefully. *Do not attempt to do yourself any steps that require the help of an adult.*

- If your project does not work properly the first time, try again or try doing it in a slightly different way. In real life, experiments don't always work out perfectly the first time.

A Word of Warning

Be sure to ask an adult to help you when the activity calls for adult help. Don't forget to get an adult's permission to use household items, and put away your equipment when you have finished. Good scientists are careful and avoid accidents.

Remember, real-life spying can be hazardous. Perform these activities only with people you know, and in safe locations.

Daring Disguises

Going Under Cover as a Spy

Spying, also called **espionage,** means observing closely and secretly. The main job of a spy is to collect secret information. If a spy is paid by her country's spy organization, called an **intelligence agency,** then the spy is a government employee called an **agent.** An agent, also called a secret agent, may be a spy catcher who tries to catch enemy spies. Or an agent may be sent on a spy mission to gather information.

When an intelligence agency sends an agent on a secret mission, the agent will often take on a **cover,** a disguise to protect her identity and motives. A spy using a cover is said to be **under cover.** An undercover spy can be a **mole,** a person who works in an enemy organization for a long time before beginning to collect secret information. A spy can also be a **double agent,** a person who spies for both sides.

Whatever a spy's mission is, science plays a big role in getting the job done. Try the following activities to learn more about spy science and how it's involved in becoming a secret agent.

Project 1

Covers

A spy under cover will often wear a disguise. Try the following activity to make your own disguise.

MATERIALS

full-length mirror

wig

sunglasses

comb or hairbrush

various old clothes (shirt, pants, hat, etc.)

1 Look at yourself in the mirror. How does your appearance make you special? What can you do to change your appearance, using the materials you have?

2 Put on the wig. How does changing your hair color or style affect your appearance?

3 Put on the sunglasses. What effect do they have on your appearance?

4 Take off the wig, then use the comb or hairbrush to change your hairstyle. If you normally wear your hair forward, comb or brush it back. Part your hair differently. How do these changes affect how you look?

5 Stand up as straight and tall as you can. Then, slump your shoulders forward, making yourself appear smaller.

6 Put on loose clothes, then tight clothes. How do they change your appearance?

7 Put on clothes with vertical (up-and-down) stripes, then clothes with horizontal (side-to-side) stripes. What effect do the stripes have?

8 Wear two layers of clothes. How does that affect your appearance?

MORE FUN STUFF TO DO

With an adult's permission, invite your friends to a disguise party. Ask each person to come to the party disguised as someone else. Not only must your guests dress their parts, they have to act them as well. They should research their characters' backgrounds. For example, if a friend comes disguised as a science teacher, he should know what a science teacher does and what a science teacher would talk about.

EXPLANATION

There are many ways to change your appearance. In this activity you explored different ways to disguise your age, height, weight, and other characteristics. Layered and loose-fitting clothes make you look heavier. Vertical stripes make you look taller, while horizontal stripes make you look wider. A wig changes your hair color and style, and large, dark sunglasses hide parts of your face.

When you slump your shoulders forward, you seem shorter. When asked later, the observer might say that you are several inches (centimeters) shorter than you really are. This is because when we first look at someone else, we retain a first impression of that person. That impression is compared to our memories and knowledge. For example, if you see a man walking hunched over, you might think he is old because you have seen other old people walk hunched over. Your memories and thoughts about how old people walk give you a bias. A **bias** is an opinion or judgment that may or may not match the facts. A bias may make it difficult to change a first impression.

Like spies, scientists know how important it is to avoid biases. If scientists allow their own opinions and ideas to affect how they view the results of an experiment, those biases may cause them to draw a false conclusion. Scientists, like spies, must always keep an open mind and be ready for unexpected information.

Lia de Beaumont may have had one of the most successful disguises in the history of spying. When presented at the eighteenth-century Russian court, Empress Elizabeth was so taken with the shy, sweet Lia that she made her a maid of honor. The empress never suspected that beneath the flowing gown, the makeup, and the wig was Charles-Geneviève-Louis-Auguste-André-Timothée d'Éon de Beaumont, a male French spy.

Spies have used many different disguises and covers to protect their identity. Perhaps the most innocent cover was adopted by Robert Baden-Powell, an Englishman. Before World War I, he traveled throughout the Austro-Hungarian Empire, posing as a **lepidopterist,** a scientist who studies butterflies. He spent his time not only chasing butterflies, but also scouting and sketching military installations. Baden-Powell is remembered for more than his work as a spy. He founded the Boy Scouts.

Legends

Project

2

To take on a cover, spies have to do more than change their looks. They have to actually act out the part. This becomes part of a spy's **legend,** the story that supports the cover she has chosen. Try the following activity to learn techniques for pretending to be someone else.

MATERIALS

scissors
several sheets of paper
pencil
several helpers

1 Cut each sheet of paper in half twice.

2 On several half sheets of paper, write an adjective describing a particular emotion, such as "angry," "happy," "sad," or "bored."

3 Gather your helpers together in a circle. Put the pieces of paper facedown in the center of the circle.

4 Ask one person to select one piece of paper and then look at the word on the paper without letting anyone else see it.

5 Have the helper act out the word without speaking, while the others try to guess what the word is.

6 After the word is correctly identified, let someone else take a turn. Continue until everyone has participated.

MORE FUN STUFF TO DO

Try writing other categories of words on the remaining pieces of paper. For example, instead of adjectives describing emotions, write types of jobs, such as "police officer," "doctor," "teacher," or "carpenter." Are these words easier or harder to act out?

EXPLANATION

Exchanging information, or **communicating,** involves more than just speech. Facial expressions and body language reveal as much about who we are as what we say does. **Behavioral scientists,** scientists who study how people act in certain situations, have discovered that body language may even be more important than speech. For example, if a person is yelling and waving her arms, yet saying she isn't angry, her actions will speak louder than her words. You'll probably think she is angry, despite what she says.

Actors have learned to make their actions reinforce their words so that audiences can both see and feel what the actors are saying. Good secret agents use the same techniques. When they take on a cover, such as that of a police officer, they make sure that their actions are similar to the way a real police officer would act.

There are two parts of any secret agent's identity. The cover is the disguise that she adopts. This involves her physical appearance and the job that she takes. The second part, her legend, is the personal life history that supports her cover. Part of her legend may be true, or all of it may be made up. However, the legend must match the cover, and the secret agent must know enough about her cover and legend to be believable. An agent will usually avoid a profession for which she is not qualified. For example, if she says she is a doctor, she may actually be asked to perform an operation.

Lafayette Baker was a spy who created an interesting cover but failed to pay enough attention to his legend. During the Civil War, he passed himself off as a traveling photographer. He roamed through Confederate military units, gathering information for the Union army.

Eventually the Confederates caught on and arrested Baker. How did they know he was a spy? They became suspicious because his job was taking pictures but he never produced any. He couldn't; his camera was broken. With a little more attention to detail, he might have gone on spying undetected for a long time.

James Rivington and Robert Townsend were excellent spies who knew how to maintain their covers. During the American Revolutionary War, they became partners in a coffeehouse in New York. Both men acted as if they were loyal to the king and spoke often of the dastardly deeds being done by the Revolutionaries. In fact, both men were secret agents who worked for General George Washington—agents so secret that neither knew the other was a spy.

Project 3
Secret Codes and Passwords

Secret agents use secret codes and passwords to identify themselves when they are under cover. But codes and passwords are also used by ordinary people every day. Try the following activity to see how they are used.

MATERIALS

sheet of paper

pencil

several adult helpers

1 Ask the adult helpers to write down the places where they use secret codes or passwords, but not the codes or passwords themselves. For example, they might use secret codes to access their bank accounts from automated teller machines (ATMs), or they might use passwords to log on to computer systems.

2 Try to guess the codes or passwords. Can you figure them out?

E X P L A N A T I O N

Most people choose codes or passwords that are easy for them to remember. People often choose the name of a friend or relative, or even a favorite sports team, as a password. Banks usually require that people choose a code number to use when accessing their bank accounts from an ATM. For this number, people often select their own birthday or the birthday of a family member.

Although such words and numbers are easy to remember, they are also easy to figure out. If you choose an easily remembered number, you should also include an unusual number or letter. For example, if your birthday is July 11, 1912 (that's my dad's birthday), rather than use the number 71112 for the code, use 711T12. The *T* in the middle of the number makes it more difficult to discover.

SPY SCIENCE IN ACTION

Author Graham Greene served as a spy on the African coast during World War II. His job was to keep an eye on an important shipping lane, an ocean path that ships usually travel, and to report any German submarine activity that he saw. He would usually sign his reports with his code name, *59200*. However, he also signed some reports using the names of various characters from classic novels.

2 Tricks of the Trade

Mastering Spy Skills and Techniques

The purpose of a spy mission, called an **operation**, is to discover information. During an operation a spy may need to get secret information about an enemy organization, or he might have to follow a person suspected of spying. In some ways, a spy operation can be like a scientific investigation. Scientists perform experiments to discover new and important information. Spies on a mission do many of the same activities that scientists do when performing experiments: they observe, compare, use numbers, predict, interpret data, and draw **inferences,** or conclusions. Spies also use many skills and techniques based on scientific principles. Try the activities in this chapter to learn some of the important spy science tricks of the trade.

Project 1

Quick Thinking

One essential trait that all spies have is their ability to think on their feet, to use their creativity and intelligence to get the information they need or to escape tricky situations. Try the following activity to test your creativity.

MATERIALS

wire coat hanger
watch or clock

PROCEDURE

1 Look at the coat hanger for 2 minutes, thinking of as many ideas as you can for what the coat hanger could become.

2 After thinking of all the possibilities, use the coat hanger to make one of the objects you thought about. You can bend the coat hanger, but you cannot add any other objects.

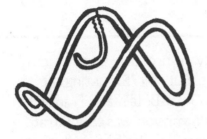

MORE FUN STUFF TO DO

Repeat the activity, using five or six common objects together. For example, use several paper clips, a rubber band, a small piece of wood, some thumbtacks, a thread spool, and a few 3-by-5-inch (7.5-by-12.5-cm) index cards to see what things you can make.

EXPLANATION

You can make many different things from the coat hanger or from the objects in the **More Fun Stuff to Do** activity. For example, the coat hanger could be bent so that it becomes a book holder, a back scratcher, or even a work of art. The objects in **More Fun Stuff to Do** might be used to build a windmill or a vehicle.

This activity shows how you can use your own creativity and imagination to turn ordinary objects into something else. When you use creativity and imagination to solve a problem, you are using **creative thinking.** Creative thinking is an important skill for spies, scientists, and really just about everyone in the world. It's a skill that can be improved by doing simple activities like these. As a secret agent, this kind of thinking can get you out of many tough situations.

SPY SCIENCE IN ACTION

Giovanni Giacomo Casanova is probably best remembered as a great ladies' man. But in 1757, during the Seven Years' War between Great Britain and France, he was a spy for the French. His mission was to **infiltrate** (to enter for secret purposes) the English fleet at Dunkirk and report on its strength.

His method was simple. Once in Dunkirk, Casanova ate at restaurants where the captains of the English fleet ate. He engaged them in conversations about ships, claiming to have once been in the navy, and entertained them with stories of his romances. In less than a week, several captains had invited him to dinner on the ships and often asked him to stay afterward. In two weeks, Casanova had learned all there was to know about the fleet and was well fed as well.

Project 2 Internet Intrigue

There are many ways to get information. With the growing popularity of computers and the Internet, secret agents can get more and more information without even leaving home. If you have a computer at home or at school with a connection to the Internet, try the following activity to see what information you can find.

computer

modem and software to connect to the Internet

adult helper

NOTE: Get an adult's permission to use the computer. Then have the adult help you with this activity if you are unfamiliar with using the computer.

1 Use your local server to connect your computer to the Internet.

2 Use a browser such as Netscape, Mosaic, or Telnet to gain access to the World Wide Web.

3 Look for information on a home page. Several U.S. government intelligence agencies have home pages that are easily accessible through browsers. Some of these are listed here:

    a. United States Intelligence Community
        http://www.odci.gov/ic/

    b. Central Intelligence Agency
        http://www.odci.gov/cia/

    c. Defense Intelligence Agency
        http://www.odci.gov/ic/usic/dia.html

    d. The White House
        http://www.whitehouse.gov

4 If you have a Net search program, such as Lycos, Infoseek, or WebCrawler, use it to search keywords, such as *espionage,* or *spies.*

Try surfing the Net for other intelligence agencies.
Can you find agencies in foreign countries?

EXPLANATION

The **Internet** is an *inter*connected *net*work that links computers
all over the world through telephone lines. A home computer
uses a modem attached to the telephone line and special software to gain access to the Internet. A **modem** is a device that
converts the messages and commands on your computer screen
into electronic data that can travel through the telephone lines
to other computers. When the data arrive at their destination,
another modem attached to a computer reverses the process

and converts the data back into a message that appears on that computer screen. Your message is received in the same form as it appeared on your screen.

Access to the Internet usually goes through a local server. A **server** is a large computer, run by a company called a provider, that makes it possible for home computers to connect to the Internet. Once connected to the Net, the home computer uses a special program called a **browser** to search for information on the World Wide Web. The **World Wide Web** is a collection of documents on the Internet that contain information provided by government agencies, businesses, and educational institutions from around the world. The first page of a Web document is called a **home page,** or Web site.

A browser acts like the card catalog in a library. It will look for a keyword throughout the Web and will tell you where to go for the information. With millions of home pages and other destinations on the World Wide Web, the browser acts like a road map, guiding you to the proper destination. With such a guide, you can gain information from just about anywhere in the world.

Trash Treasures

Secret agents have many high-tech ways to gather information about a person. But they also often get valuable information out of the trash. Try the following activity to see how it's done.

MATERIALS

rubber gloves

several sheets of newspaper

trash can filled with trash

pencil

sheet of paper

CAUTION: Do not use a trash can containing old food.

1 Put on the rubber gloves and spread the newspaper out on the floor.

2 Take the trash out of the can and place it on the newspaper.

3 Sort the trash into piles of similar items. For example, you might have a pile for papers and letters, a pile for containers (like soda cans and Styrofoam cups), and a pile for miscellaneous items.

4 Write down the items in each pile. Next to each item, note what it tells you about the people who use that trash can. For example, an empty Styrofoam coffee cup from a coffee shop might suggest that your teacher visited that coffee shop and likes to drink coffee. The return address on an envelope addressed to your mom tells you that she knows someone who lives at a certain address in another city. What other things does the trash tell you?

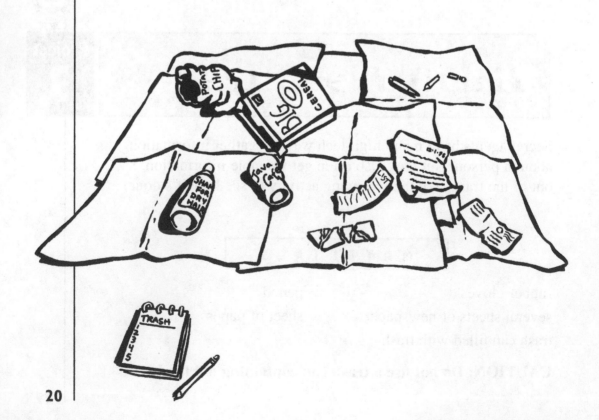

MORE FUN STUFF TO DO

With permission, try going through trash cans from several different people's bedrooms. Can you match the trash cans to the people they came from? How accurately does this type of information describe the people?

EXPLANATION

Believe it or not, going through the trash is a procedure done by both intelligence agencies and the police. The items that a person discards can often provide important clues about him. These clues can serve as the basis of a **hypothesis** (an educated guess or theory) that can be tested with further investigation.

This type of work is similar to the work of an archaeologist. An **archaeologist** is a scientist who learns about cultures from the past by studying their remains. Garbage is a source of many **artifacts,** objects that were used by people in the past. A coin or vase can reveal much about the people who lived in a certain area. For example, a coin may have a date on it that links an ancient city with the time it was occupied. Words on the coin indicate the writing system of the society. A vase may have images on it that give an indication of how the people looked and dressed. From the information provided by artifacts, archaeologists can also form hypotheses about how people lived in the past. These hypotheses may later be proved or disproved by the discovery of other artifacts.

Mikhail Gorin was a Russian working in the United States in 1938. His job was arranging tours of America for Russian tourists. But trash found in his pockets revealed that he was a spy. Gorin had sent his suit to the dry cleaner's to be cleaned. A worker at the cleaner's checked the pockets of the suit before cleaning it and found a $50 bill. The worker was about to call Gorin to tell him about the bill, when he discovered several other sheets of crumpled paper. The sheets contained notes concerning Japanese spies on the West Coast. The worker called the Federal Bureau of Investigation (FBI) instead, and Gorin was arrested.

Project 4

Opening Letters

A spy needs many ways of getting information without being caught. A spy might want to read a letter addressed to someone else without that person knowing. Try the following activity to use science to open envelopes.

MATERIALS

pencil

sheet of paper

envelope

teakettle filled with water

stove (to be used only by an adult)

oven mitt

tongs

watch or clock

adult helper

NOTE: This activity requires adult help.

1. Write a message on the sheet of paper, then seal it in the envelope.

2. Ask an adult to put the teakettle on the stove, heat it until the water boils, then reduce the heat to medium.

3. Wearing the oven mitt, pick up the tongs.

4. With adult supervision, use the tongs to hold the envelope. Carefully place the sealed flap of the envelope in front of the steam coming from the spout of the kettle. Hold it there for 30 seconds.

5. After 30 seconds, remove the envelope and try to open the flap. If you cannot open it, return the envelope to the steam and wait another 30 seconds. Continue this process until you are able to open the envelope and read the message.

MORE FUN STUFF TO DO

Repeat the procedure, only this time after you seal the envelope, place a piece of transparent tape over the flap. Try to open the taped envelope using steam.

EXPLANATION

The glue on the flap of the envelope is made of a chemical that is **water soluble,** meaning it **dissolves,** or becomes liquid, in water. When you lick the envelope flap, the glue dissolves, forming a sticky liquid. After you seal the envelope, the water **evaporates** (changes from a liquid to a gas), causing the glue to change from a sticky liquid back to a solid. The glue hardens, sealing the flap of the envelope, and the letter remains closed.

When you boil water it changes rapidly from a liquid to a gas. Water's gas form is called **water vapor.** It is invisible. However, the water vapor **condenses** (changes from a gas to a liquid) as it cools, changing to tiny droplets of water called **steam.**

When you put the envelope in the steam from the boiling kettle, the steam causes the glue to dissolve again and become sticky. You can then open the flap on the envelope and read the letter. After you have read the letter, you can put it back in the envelope, reseal it, and send it on its way. There are no signs that the envelope has been opened.

Transparent tape is the best-known protection against opening letters. The glue on transparent tape is not water soluble. So far, no way has been found to remove the tape from an envelope and replace it without leaving telltale marks.

Tailing

An agent often has to **tail,** or closely follow, a person in order to gain information. Tailing a person will tell an agent of the person's habits and daily routines. Although this may seem trivial at first, it often leads to more valuable information later. Try the following activity to test your ability to tail someone.

MATERIALS

notebook
pen or pencil
watch
several helpers

PROCEDURE

1. Gather several helpers together. Inform them that at some point during the next week, you are going to tail one of them as part of your experiment. (Telling them that you are going to tail them makes your task more difficult but will avoid embarrassment.)

CAUTION: Tail the person at school or in another safe location, such as a party. Never wander around alone.

2. Choose a day and select one person to follow for 1 hour. Use a notebook to record notes of his activities and any people he encounters. Record the time for all notes you make.

3 When you finish tailing the person, review your notes. Are there any activities that surprised you? Could you tell exactly what happened during each encounter with other people? Did the person figure out that you were tailing him?

 MORE FUN STUFF TO DO

Agents seldom follow a suspect by themselves. They usually work in teams to prevent the suspect from getting suspicious. Often a second, third, or even a fourth agent will pick up the tail where the previous agent leaves off. Try using a team to tail one of your helpers.

It is difficult to tail a person without being noticed. If the person being followed sees the same person, especially a stranger, over and over again, it seems unusual. The person's brain is alerted that something out of the ordinary has happened. He will become more cautious and will try to see if someone is indeed tailing him. This is why agents use teams to follow people. One agent will follow the suspect for a short time, then a second, third, or even a fourth agent will pick up the tail. The person being followed does not see the same person, so his brain is not alerted that something unusual is happening.

Tailing a suspect is a form of surveillance. **Surveillance** is a close watch kept over someone or something. Secret agents practice surveillance for many reasons. Agents may watch a person's home or place of work in order to gain information or even to catch the person spying. Or they may tail a person to get information about the person's habits, daily routine, people contacted, place of work, home address, or type of transportation.

A secret agent can use the information gathered from tailing someone to form a hypothesis or theory about that person, just as a scientist uses information to form a hypothesis about an experiment. For example, an agent might observe a man working in the president's office who meets with a woman and passes slips of paper to her at the same time every day. The agent might hypothesize that the office worker is spying on the president and that the papers are secret information he collects and passes on each day.

The truth may be that the office worker is meeting his girlfriend and passing love notes. Or he could be passing on information that is very valuable to foreign countries, such as facts about a plan the president is considering to stop a war or details of a treaty being negotiated. The agent will continue to investigate to determine which hypothesis is correct, in the same way that a scientist will test a hypothesis through experimentation.

Mapping

Whether a spy is at home or in foreign territory, she must know her exact location. Mapping skills are very important tools for a secret agent. Try pretending that your school or home is a secret organization, and make a map of it.

MATERIALS

measuring tape
sheet of paper
pencil

PROCEDURE

1 Unroll the measuring tape and lay it faceup on the floor.

2 Place the big toe of your right foot at the zero mark of the tape, and take one step with your left foot. Record the length from the big toe of your right foot to the big toe of your left foot. This is the length of one of your footsteps.

3 Begin your map by making a drawing of the outside of your school or house. Is it a square, a rectangle, or another shape?

4 Count out and write down how many steps it takes you to walk the length of each side of the building.

5 Multiply the number of steps for each side of the building by the length of your footstep to determine the length. Record the measurements on your map.

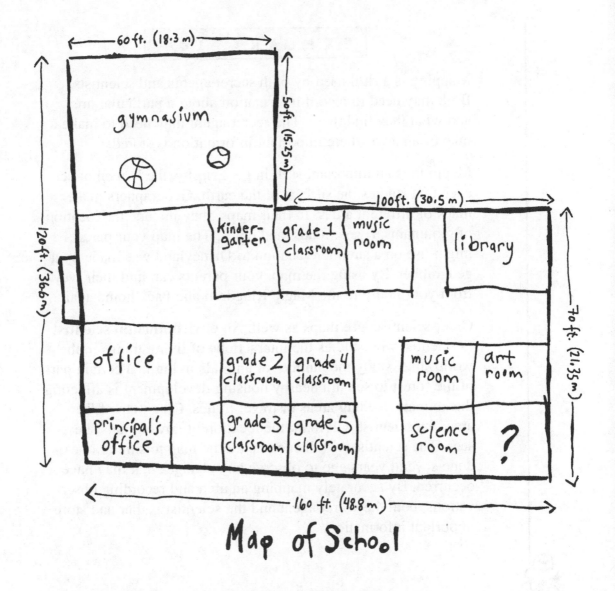

Map of School

6   Fill in the inside of the building. How many rooms
    are there? Do you know what each room is used for?
    Record the information on your map. (If there are locked
    doors in the school, try to find out what the rooms are
    used for.)

7   When you are finished, look at the completed map. How
    accurate is it? Were you able to get all the information
    that you needed?

Mapping is a skill used by both secret agents and scientists. Both may need to record information about a particular area and what they find there. The secret agent may need to make a map of an area where important information is stored.

Mapping is an important skill in **geography,** the branch of science that studies the surface of the earth. Geographers make maps of different areas. In their maps, they include the location of mountains, rivers, roads, and cities. The map your parents might use on a summer vacation to Disneyland was made by a geographer. By using the map, your parents can find their way from your house to the Magic Kingdom and back home again.

Other scientists use maps as well. An **environmental scientist** (a scientist who studies the interactions of living things in the world) may study the number of animals living in a certain part of the forest to see if a nearby housing development is affecting the animals' feeding areas or travel routes. On a map of the area, the scientist will mark the location of any animals she sees. The scientist will then compare the map to similar ones done several years ago to observe any changes that may have occurred. By accurately mapping an area and recording observations, both the secret agent and the scientist gather and store important information.

Project 7

Mock Compass

You're a spy on the run and enemy agents are close behind. You know that your meeting point is due north, but you don't have a compass. Which way do you go? Try the following activity and learn a way to find north without a compass.

watch with hands (a digital watch won't work)
toothpick

NOTE: This activity must be performed outdoors on a sunny day.

1 Standing in a sunny spot, hold the watch faceup in the palm of your hand.

2 With your other hand, hold the toothpick in the center of the watch so that it casts a shadow on the face of the watch.

3 Turn the watch so that the shadow from the toothpick falls across the hour hand of the watch.

4 Imagine a line going from the center of the watch halfway between the hour hand and the number 12. For example, if the hour hand is directly on the 10, as it would be at 10 o'clock, the imaginary line would be halfway between 10 and 12, or at 11.

5 Locate the direction north by facing in the direction of the imaginary line.

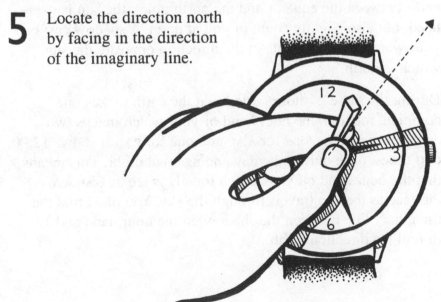

Try to think of other ways that you could find your way without a compass. How else could you find north? What if you were traveling at night?

EXPLANATION

During the 24 hours that make up a day (and night), the earth makes one full **rotation** (turn) on its axis. Although it's actually the earth that moves, from our view on earth, the sun appears to travel across the sky. Each day, the sun rises in the east and sets in the west. If you place a stick in the ground on a sunny day, watch its shadow move, and mark the shadow's location each hour, the result would be a simple sundial. You could use the sundial to tell time the next day by looking at the location of the shadow and comparing it to the previous day's marks. This same basic principle explains how you can use a watch to find north.

Each day, the sun is in the same general direction in the sky at noon. If you live in the **Northern Hemisphere** (the half of the earth between the equator and the north pole), the sun is overhead, but also slightly south of you at noon. A shadow cast on your watch at noon points in the direction opposite the sun, which is north.

During the same 24-hour period that the earth makes one complete rotation, the hour hand of your watch makes two complete rotations, one for A.M. and one for P.M. It shows 12:00 two times, once during the day and again at night. This means that the hour hand on your watch travels twice as fast across the face as the sun travels through the sky. You must find the imaginary line between the shadow on the hour hand and 12 to find the direction north.

You are a spy working under cover. You have figured out a way to obtain the key to a locked room, but must return it in a short time. You want to make a quick copy of the key so you can explore the room at a later time. What can you do? Try the following activity to see how it can be done.

MATERIALS

sheet of black construction paper
4 rocks
key
clock or watch

PROCEDURE

NOTE: This activity must be performed outdoors on a sunny day.

1 Place the construction paper in an open area in bright sunlight. Place a rock on each corner of the paper so that the wind will not blow it away.

2 Place the key in the center of the paper.

3 Leave the project in the sun for at least 4 hours.

4 Remove the key and observe the paper. What do you see?

 MORE FUN STUFF TO DO

Try leaving the key on the paper for periods of time longer and shorter than 4 hours. How long does the paper need to be in the sun for the key to leave an imprint? Try the experiment on a partly sunny day. Does the key leave an imprint?

EXPLANATION

Paper is made from wood **fibers** (slender threadlike structures that give woody plants strength) that have been pressed together. Construction paper gets its color from different dyes. When construction paper is made, particles of dye dissolved in water **bond** (join together by an attractive force) to the paper fibers in a chemical reaction. A **chemical reaction** is a change in matter in which substances break apart to form new substances. A different chemical reaction occurs when sunlight hits the paper, causing the paper to fade, or lose its color.

All colored paper will eventually fade if exposed to sunlight. You may have noticed this on the bulletin board at school. Areas that have been covered by pictures are darker colored than surrounding areas when the pictures are removed.

Colored paper fades even more quickly in direct sunlight. Black construction paper in particular fades very fast, because it contains the most dyes. The key, or any other object, blocks the sun and keeps the area under it from fading. After a short time, the rest of the paper fades, leaving an exact imprint of the key on the paper. You then have a picture of the key. An experienced spy could make a copy of the key and return the key to the locked room later.

Watch the Birdie

Project 9

A secret agent may need to take photographs during his mission. How can the agent take a photograph without being noticed? Try the following activity to learn a special spy method.

MATERIALS

section of newspaper, folded in half

scissors

camera

helper

NOTE: Get an adult's permission before using the camera.

1 Unfold the section of the newspaper. Cut a hole in the middle of the top half of the section, through all the pages. The hole should be big enough for the camera lens to fit through.

2 Position the camera inside the newspaper so that the lens sticks out through the hole.

3 Refold the newspaper with the camera inside.

4 Practice aiming the camera, putting your hand inside the newspaper to push the button to take the picture.

5 After you have practiced, take a picture of your helper without his knowing.

MORE FUN STUFF TO DO

What other ways can you hide a camera in order to take a photograph without being detected?

A newspaper is a good place in which to hide a camera, because it is an ordinary object. A secret agent could conceal his camera inside the newspaper and not cause suspicion when walking near a weapons factory. With the hidden camera, he could take photographs without anyone's noticing.

Photography is a process of producing images of objects on a special surface, such as film. A camera **focuses** (brings together) the correct amount of light from an object onto chemicals called silver salts found on the surface of film. When light hits the surface of film, a chemical reaction occurs. This reaction changes the silver salts black, creating a negative image of the object. The negative is then placed in a fixing solution, which dissolves the unaffected silver salts from the film and prevents any further reaction with light. A negative looks opposite to real life because light areas appear dark and dark areas appear light.

A photograph is then made from a negative. Light is passed through the negative and an enlarger. A **magnified** (enlarged) image from the negative then falls on a piece of special printing paper that is also light sensitive, producing a photograph. The photograph looks like real life because the dark areas of the negative become light and the light areas of the negative become dark.

Hiding Places

Project
10

It often takes several days or even months for a secret agent to obtain all the information that she might need. She might have to hold on to the information until her next meeting. What should she do with the information? Try the following activity and see how good you are at hiding information.

small paperback book
helper

P R O C E D U R E

1 Show the small book to the helper. Tell her that you are going to hide the book somewhere in the room.

2 Ask your helper to leave the room. Then, hide the book.

3 Have your helper return to the room and search for the book until she finds it. If your helper is having difficulty, you can give hints, such as "getting warmer" when she moves closer to the book and "getting colder" when she moves farther away.

4 After your helper has found the book, have her hide the book while you try to find it.

Try hiding other objects, such as a piece of paper or a photograph. Are all objects easy to hide? Where are the best hiding places?

EXPLANATION

There are many ways to hide an object. A book is fairly large and can be easily found. If the object is small, it is often more difficult to find. Certain objects can be hidden in plain sight. For example, a piece of paper can be hidden in a book, because the pages of a book are also paper. If the hidden information is on a page that is the same size and same type as the pages in a book, then it is doubly difficult to find. But be careful if you put the book in a library: the hidden message may be hidden forever.

Gotcha!

Project 11

You are a spy, working under cover in a foreign city. You begin to suspect that you are being followed and that your apartment will soon be searched. What do you do? How will you know if your room has been entered while you were out? Try the following activity to find out.

MATERIALS

toothpick

1   When you leave your room, hold the toothpick between the door and the doorjamb as you close the door so that part of the toothpick sticks out between the door and the doorjamb.

2   Shut the door tight and break off the part of the toothpick that is sticking out. Put the piece of toothpick you have broken off in your pocket. The piece that remains in the door is your "Gotcha!" alarm system.

3   Leave. If the toothpick is not in its place when you return, you know your room has been entered.

Challenge someone to try to enter your room secretly while you are out without your discovering it. With your "Gotcha!" alarm system, you should be able to tell if anyone enters.

EXPLANATION

If anyone other than you enters your room, the toothpick will fall to the floor. Someone entering might not notice, but when you return, you will quickly see that the toothpick is no longer stuck in the door. Even if the person does notice the fallen toothpick, he will not be able to replace the toothpick with a different one without your knowing it. The broken end of the new toothpick will not match the one you are carrying.

Toothpicks are made of wood **fibers** of various lengths that are randomly arranged. When you break apart the toothpick, the fibers separate. Since no two toothpicks have fibers that are identical in length and arrangement, all toothpicks will break differently. Even if you tried, you could not make identical breaks in two toothpicks. The end of a broken toothpick is unique and can be perfectly matched to the end of the other half.

Hairy Situation

Project 12

There are other ways that spies know if others have searched their rooms. Investigators routinely search books. Books may contain secret messages trapped between the pages. Try the next activity to learn a way to tell if someone has been looking through your books.

book

strand of human hair

1   Open the book to a specific page, one that you can remember.

2   Place the hair on the center of the page so that one end of the hair extends past the edge of the pages.

3   Carefully close the book so that you do not disturb the hair. Place the book on a table or desk in your room. Leave your room, knowing that you will be able to tell if anyone has looked through your books.

MORE FUN STUFF TO DO

Dust is another thing that can be used to detect searches. With an adult's permission, slap two chalk erasers together over your desk or dresser. This will leave a layer of fine dust that will show any disturbance made by someone searching your room and its contents.

EXPLANATION

A strand of human hair is very light. Even the slightest breeze can cause it to move. Anyone who opens the book will move the hair. It is very unlikely that someone looking through your books will even notice the hair. If she does notice the hair, she will have a hard time replacing it exactly as it was. Spies often adopt a characteristic way of positioning hair, which is their trademark.

Dust can also reveal when something has been touched. Slight disturbances show up clearly on a dusty surface. Once the dusty surface is disturbed, it is very difficult to put the dust back. Secret agents use powdered chalk, colored to match the surface it is on, to check whether something has been touched or moved. If you are an agent investigating a spy and you know that she uses the colored-chalk method of detection, the only way to cover your tracks is to wipe the whole area clean and apply a new coat of the same kind of chalk.

3

Magical Gadgets

Building Spy Tools and Devices

Many spy operations use gadgets or devices to help gather information. Spies have special gadgets that let them watch others without being seen, and devices that let them listen in on conversations in other rooms. Spies use **bugs**—not the kind that live in your garden, but tiny recording devices that can be hidden almost anywhere and can **transmit,** or send, conversations hundreds of yards (meters) away. Spies may use night-vision goggles to let them see clearly in the dark, or digital voice changers that fit over the mouthpiece of a telephone and disguise the spy's voice.

All the devices spies use, from very basic to very high-tech, use science to help them get the information they need. Try the activities in this chapter to discover and make your own amazing espionage objects.

Project 1: Seeing around Corners

It is difficult to spy on someone without being seen. Secret agents use devices that allow them to hide behind objects, such as buildings or trees, and still be able to observe someone. Build a device called a periscope to see without being seen.

MATERIALS

scissors

two 1-quart (1-liter) cardboard milk cartons (empty and clean)

transparent tape

ruler

protractor

pencil

2 small mirrors at least 3 inches (7.5 cm) square (available cut to size at many glass stores)

1 Cut off the top and bottom of each milk carton.

2 Tape the two cartons together end to end so that they form a long tube.

3 Place the tube upright on a table. Cut a 2-inch (5-cm) -square opening in one side of one end of the tube. Cut another 2-inch (5-cm) -square opening in the opposite side of the other end of the tube as shown.

4 With the protractor, measure 45-degree angles on the sides adjacent to each square. To do this, place the center of the protractor on the corner of one end of the tube, next to the side with the square opening. Use the pencil to make a mark on the tube at 45 degrees. Use the ruler to draw a line from the corner of the tube to the mark. Repeat for the corner next to the other square opening.

5 Cut two ⅛-by-3-inch (0.31-by-7.5-cm) slots along the 45-degree marks.

6 Slide the mirrors into the slots. The shiny sides must face each other. Tape the mirrors to the tube to hold them in place. You have made a periscope.

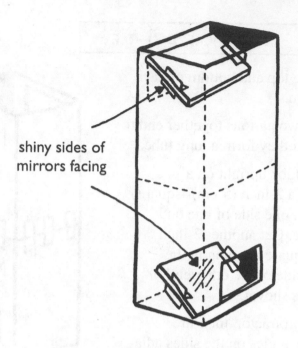

shiny sides of
mirrors facing

7 Hold your tube upright, and look into one of the square openings. You should be able to see over the heads of people or things that are taller than you. If you hold your periscope sideways, you'll be able to see around corners.

MORE FUN STUFF TO DO

Camouflage (disguise) your periscope so that it is not easily seen. If you will be spying from behind bushes, glue or tape leaves onto the periscope. If you plan to spy from behind a building, use crayons or markers to make the periscope the same color as the building.

EXPLANATION

A **periscope** is a device that uses mirrors to allow you to see around corners and above your head. The mirrors reflect light, which is a form of energy that travels in a straight line. When light hits a flat mirror, it **reflects** (bounces off) the mirror at an angle equal to the angle at which it went in.

The periscope works by using two flat mirrors. The image you see reflects off one mirror and onto the other mirror at an equal angle, and then reflects off the second mirror and onto the lens of your eye. The **lens** is the part of your eye that focuses light at one point inside your eyeball. The image that results is called a **point retinal image.** Thus you are able to see a clear image of objects out of your sight.

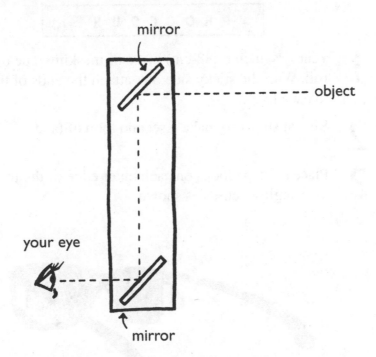

Seeing behind You

You're spying on someone and want to watch her without drawing suspicion. Secret agents use several devices to help them. Try the following activity to build one device they use.

ruler

masking tape

sunglasses (large dark or mirrored glasses work best)

2 small 1-by-½-inch (2.5-by-1.25-cm) mirrors
  (available cut to size at many glass stores)

PROCEDURE

1 Tear a ¾-inch (1.88-cm) piece of masking tape off the roll. With the sticky side out, attach the ends of the tape to make a loop.

2 Repeat step 1 to make a second loop of tape.

3 Place the tape loops on each outer edge of the inside of the sunglass lenses as shown.

4 Stick the mirrors to the tape.

5 Put on the sunglasses. By glancing at the mirrors, you should be able to see behind you.

Like the periscope that uses mirrors to allow you to see above your head and around corners, the sunglasses use mirrors to allow you to see behind you. Mirrors work by reflecting light. The mirrors on the sides of the sunglasses reflect the light from objects behind you. The light reflects off the flat mirror at an angle equal to the angle at which it went in. The light hits the lens of your eye and is focused inside your eyeball as a clear image. You are then able to see the objects behind you.

Seeing It All

Project

3

You've seen ways that spies can see around corners, above their heads, and behind them, but can they see through walls as well? Try the following activity to investigate one way secret agents can improve their spy vision.

MATERIALS

scissors

ruler

sheet of black construction paper

clear glass marble at least ½ inch (1.25 cm) in **diameter** (the length of a line passing through the center of a circle)

PROCEDURE

1. Cut the sheet of construction paper into an 8½-by-5½-inch (22-by-14-cm) rectangle.

2 Roll the paper into a 5½-inch (14-cm) -long tube the same **circumference** (the distance around a circle) as the marble.

3 Stand in front of a window and look out the window through the tube. How much of the world outside your window can you see?

4 Place the marble in one end of the tube so that half the marble is in the tube and half is sticking out the end as shown. You may have to adjust the paper tube so that the marble is held firmly in place.

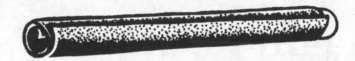

5 Look out the window through the open end of the tube. How much of the world outside your window can you see now? What does it look like?

MORE FUN STUFF TO DO

Repeat the activity with marbles of different sizes. Does the image of the area that you see change?

EXPLANATION

When you look out the window through the empty paper tube, you can only see a little bit of the world outside. When you place the marble in the end of the tube, you can suddenly see much, much more. That is because the marble acts like a lens. A

lens is a curved piece of glass or other transparent substance that **refracts** (bends) and focuses rays of light passing through it.

Light rays from the object you are looking at pass through the lens. Light rays going through the top and bottom of the lens are refracted more than those going through the middle of the lens. The light rays meet at a point called the **focus** of the lens. The light rays continue beyond the focus, but the image you see is **inverted** (turned upside down) because the light rays from the top of the object are now at the bottom of the image.

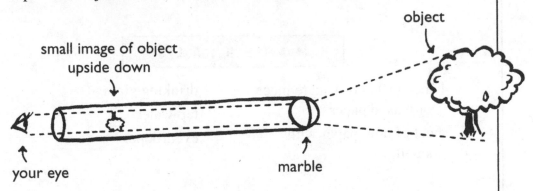

This same principle is used in peepholes, which are small holes in the front doors of apartments and some houses that allow people inside to look out. Inside the peephole is a glass lens that refracts the light from objects outside the door. The glass lens allows you to see more than you could looking out from just a small hole in the door.

Secret agents use similar devices to help them see through walls. If they want to spy on people in the next room, they drill a very small hole in the wall between the rooms. The hole is no bigger around than the lead in a pencil and is usually not noticed by the people in the room. Agents stick a small tube with a lens through the hole. The lens performs the same function as the marble in the paper tube, allowing the agents to see everything that is happening in the room. They make the image right side up by adding a second lens that again inverts the image. Often agents will connect the lens to a video camera so they can record what is happening on a VCR.

Seeing It Bigger

Spies often use magnifying lenses in their work. They may need to view secret messages written in very small print (see Chapter 4, Project 4, "Small Secrets"). How can a spy make a magnifying lens in an emergency? Try the following activity to learn how.

MATERIALS

4-inch (10-cm) -square piece
  of waxed paper

sheet of newspaper with
  small print

drinking glass

tap water

eyedropper

PROCEDURE

1 Place the square of waxed paper on top of the newspaper. Observe the newspaper through the waxed paper.

2 Fill the glass half full with water.

3 Use the eyedropper to place a tiny drop of water on the waxed paper.

4 Observe the newspaper through the drop of water. Does the printing under the drop seem larger or smaller than the printing surrounding the drop?

MORE FUN STUFF TO DO

Try making the drops smaller or larger. Does the size of the drop affect the size of the printing you see?

EXPLANATION

The drop of water forms a rounded shape on the waxed paper due to the surface tension of water. **Surface tension** is the force of attraction between water particles that creates a thin skin on the surface of the water. This rounded shape of the water drop is the same shape as a **convex lens,** which is a lens that is curved like the outside of a ball. (A **concave lens** is curved like the inside of a bowl.) When light from an object passes through a convex lens, the image of the object is **magnified.**

The smaller the drop of water, the more curved its shape and the more it magnifies an image. The larger the drop of water, the less curved it is and the less it magnifies. The weight of the larger drop of water causes it to flatten out and lose its curve.

With a larger drop of water, you can see more letters but they are less magnified than with a smaller drop.

A magnifying lens made of glass works like a water drop, but it is easier to use. A magnifying lens is a convex lens that makes the objects it magnifies seem larger than they really are.

Listening In

You're spying on two people in the next room. They're discussing their next operation, but you can't hear what they're saying. Try the following activity to make a device to hear through doors.

MATERIALS

yardstick (meterstick)
drinking glass
2 helpers

PROCEDURE

1. Meet with the helpers in a room of your house. Tell them that you are going to try to listen to what they are saying from the next room. Ask them to have a conversation in normal tones of voice, no louder or softer than usual.

2. Have your helpers stand 2 yards (2 m) away, facing the door. Leave the room and close the door.

3. Listen to the conversation. What do you hear?

4. Place the open end of the glass against the door, and place your ear against the bottom of the glass. What do you hear?

MORE FUN STUFF TO DO

With the glass against the door, have your helpers talk louder, then softer. Can you hear them both times?

Every sound you hear, including speech, is caused by vibrations. When we speak, air from our lungs rushes past the vocal cords in our throats, causing them to **vibrate** (move to and fro repeatedly). These vibrations, like all vibrations, travel through air as sound waves. Sound waves can travel through all matter —gases, liquids, and solids. In this activity, the sound waves from the voices travel through the air to the door, then through the door itself. The sound waves then become sounds you can recognize with your ears.

You hear the voices better when you place the glass to the door, because the glass acts as a cavity to **amplify** (make louder) the sound. The sound waves inside the glass cavity hit the walls of the glass, reflect back, and reinforce each other in a process called **resonance.**

SPY SCIENCE IN ACTION

On the night of December 4, 1777, the British army marched out of Philadelphia for a surprise attack on the Continental army (the American army that fought the British during the Revolutionary War), who were camped 8 miles (13 km) away.

But the Americans weren't surprised at all. They knew all about the attack and were ready. Well dug in, with cannons ready, they battled the British to a standstill. Two days later, the British army retreated to Philadelphia.

How did the Continental army know about the surprise attack? Four days earlier, the British staff officers entered the home of William and Lydia Darragh and took over one room for a council chamber. During their stay, Mrs. Darragh, a volunteer spy for the Continental army, learned of the British attack and managed to get word to the Americans in time. She did not gain the British plans by figuring out a code or **intercepting** (receiving a communication directed elsewhere) a secret message. She simply listened at the keyhole.

Don't Bug Me

There are many high-tech listening devices that secret agents can use to hear the conversations of others. A bug hidden in a room will transmit conversations taking place in the room to a device called a receiver outside the room. This activity will let you simulate making a bug and hiding it in a room.

MATERIALS

5 plastic bottle caps
five 2-inch (5-cm) squares of aluminum foil
five 4-inch (10-cm) pieces of masking tape
watch or clock
helper

PROCEDURE

1 Cover the bottle caps with the foil.

2 Make a loop with each piece of tape so that the sticky side faces out. Stick one tape loop on top of each bottle cap.

3 Have your helper leave the room for exactly 2 minutes. While the helper is gone, hide the bugs by sticking them in various hard-to-see places around the room.

4 When the helper returns, give him 5 minutes to find the bugs. If all the bugs are not found in 5 minutes, show your helper where they are.

5 Have your helper hide the bugs while you are out of the room.

 ## MORE FUN STUFF TO DO

Have several helpers try to find the bugs at once. The person who finds the most bugs gets to hide them the next time. Make it even harder by using colored paper to camouflage the bugs. Plan where you are going to hide the bugs, and cover each one in paper that matches the area where it will go.

A bug has a tiny microphone inside it that picks up the sounds of people talking. The bug also has a **transmitter,** a device that can send messages from one place to another, often using radio waves. The transmitter sends the voice sounds as radio waves to a receiver that the spy has set up outside the room. The **receiver** turns the radio waves sent by the transmitter back into sounds in the same way a radio does.

Bugs are very small and can be placed in almost any location in a room. Some are the size of the bottle caps you used in this activity. Some are even smaller. Bugs can even be hidden inside telephones to record phone calls.

Testing One, Two, Three

Project
7

Suppose you have been tailing an enemy agent to a meeting with someone you suspect is his **contact** (a person to whom a spy passes information or from whom the spy gets information). They are meeting in the middle of a grassy field. How can you hear what they are saying without getting too close? Try the following activity to learn about one of the high-tech gadgets that intelligence agencies use to gather information.

MATERIALS

yardstick (meterstick)

tape recorder with microphone

large mixing bowl (as large and as round as possible)

helper

NOTE: This activity works best in an outdoor area.

1 Have your helper walk about 20 feet (6.5 m) away from you and stay there facing you throughout the experiment.

2 Hold the microphone of the tape recorder so that it faces your helper.

3 Ask your helper to talk in a normal tone of voice while you record what he is saying.

4 Play back the recording. How well does the recording pick up the voice?

5 Hold the bowl in front of you so that the inside of the bowl faces your helper.

6 Hold the microphone so that it faces the inside of the bowl. The microphone should be at approximately the center of the bowl, at an equal distance from all sides.

7 Ask your helper to speak again in a normal tone of voice while you record what he is saying.

8 Play back the recording. How well does the recording pick up the voice this time?

MORE FUN STUFF TO DO

Repeat the activity with the bowl, only this time hold the microphone at different distances away from the bowl. Is there a place where the recording is easiest to understand?

EXPLANATION

The listening device you've made is a **parabolic microphone.** A parabolic microphone is a microphone that is attached to a parabolic reflector to amplify sound. A **parabolic reflector** is a bowl-like device that receives sounds and focuses them at one point.

In this activity, when the sound waves from your helper's voice come toward you, the waves are parallel to one another and spread out over a large area. The sound waves hit the parabolic reflector and bounce off the reflector at angles equal to the angles at which they went in. Because the parabolic reflector is

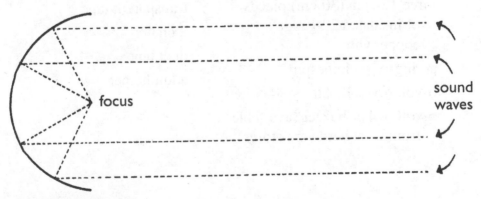

focus

sound waves

Parabolic Reflector

curved, the reflected sound waves all meet at one point, called the focus. If the microphone is put at the focus, it picks up the sound from all the waves, not just a few. Focusing the sounds at one point makes them much louder.

Parabolic microphones are used not only by secret agents, but also by film crews, bird-watchers, and sports audio recorders. To avoid the microphones' being seen, secret agents use parabolic microphones much smaller than the one you built. In high-tech parabolic microphones, the reflector is no larger than a cereal bowl.

Project 8 Alarm

You have plans to meet another secret agent at a location in your backyard, and you want to be sure that you'll know if someone tries to sneak up on you. Try the following activity to make an alarm to protect your secret meeting.

MATERIALS

wire strippers or pliers (to be used only by an adult)

ruler

three 12-inch (30-cm) pieces of insulated 22-gauge copper wire

spring-type clothespin

6-volt dry-cell battery

6-volt bell or buzzer (available from most hardware stores)

toothpick

6 feet (2 m) clear nylon fishing line

transparent tape

2 chairs

duct tape

adult helper

NOTE: This activity requires adult help. Get an adult's permission before using the chairs and duct tape.

1 Have your adult helper use the wire strippers to remove ½ inch (1.25 cm) of insulation from the ends of all three wires and an additional 1 inch (2.5 cm) from one end of two of the wires.

2 Using the wires with the additional insulation removed, wind the longer stripped ends around each jaw of the clothespin so that the wires touch when the clothespin is pinched.

3 Wrap the free end of one clothespin wire around one of the battery terminals. Wrap the free end of the other clothespin wire around one of the screw terminals of the bell.

4 Wrap one end of the third wire around the other bell screw terminal. Wrap the other end around the other battery terminal, being careful not to touch the bare wire so that you do not get a shock. The bell should sound.

5 Pinch the clothespin and place one end of the toothpick in the jaws of the clothespin. This will keep the wires apart and stop the bell from ringing.

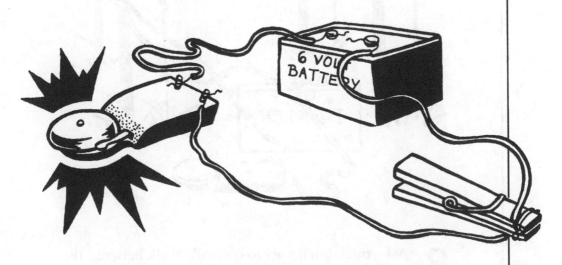

6 Tie one end of the nylon fishing line to the other end of the toothpick. Secure the fishing line to the toothpick with transparent tape.

7 Place the chairs about 4 feet (1.3 m) apart. With adult permission, use the duct tape to tape the clothespin to a leg of one chair about 6 inches (15 cm) above the ground so that the jaws of the clothespin face the other chair. Stretch the fishing line taut and tie it to a leg of the other chair at about the same height. Your alarm is now set.

CAUTION: Do not use the alarm without warning people first, as someone could trip and fall.

8 Ask your adult helper to carefully walk between the chairs. What happens?

Your alarm sounds when the toothpick is knocked out or removed, because of electricity. **Electricity** is a form of energy caused by the movement of tiny, negatively charged particles called **electrons.** In order for electrons to move, two things are needed. The first is a source of energy for the electrons. For your alarm, the energy is supplied by the chemical reaction that takes place inside the battery. The second thing needed is an **electric circuit,** a complete circular path for the electrons to travel to and from the energy source. Your alarm has an electric circuit that runs from the battery, through the wires to the bell, back through the other wires, to the opposite end of the battery.

While the toothpick is between the jaws of the clothespin, however, the electric circuit is broken by the toothpick. The electrons cannot travel through the toothpick. When the nylon fishing line pulls the toothpick out, the wires touch, closing the electric circuit between the battery and the bell. Electricity flows again from the battery to the bell and back, and your alarm sounds.

Tricycle Tracker

Project 9

It can be difficult to follow a spy in a vehicle. Traffic, stoplights, and pedestrians can all get in the way. What is a spy catcher to do? Try making the following tracking device to track a tricycle.

MATERIALS

small nail

plastic milk container
(empty and clean)

duct tape

tap water

tricycle

helper

NOTE: Get your younger brother's or sister's permission before using the tricycle and duct tape.

1 Use the nail to make a small hole in the bottom of the container, near the outer edge.

2 Place a piece of duct tape over the hole, and fill the container with water.

3 Position the container on the footrest of the tricycle so that the hole is over the ground and not on the footrest itself.

4 Use the duct tape to tape the container in place.

5 Have your helper get on the tricycle. Just before he rides off, remove the tape from the hole.

6 Have your helper ride the tricycle in a safe location. Can you follow where your helper has gone?

Your tricycle tracker is similar to a device that secret agents have used for years. Usually the container is filled with paint or another substance that can be easily seen and is placed on the spy's vehicle. When the spy drives off, the liquid leaves a trail. This type of tracking is safer than tailing the spy. In a regular tail, it is possible that the spy will notice that he is being followed and will call off the operation. By following the trail of paint, however, an agent can tell where the spy has gone without risking being seen.

This device works because of the principle that liquids flow at a constant rate out of a small hole. A small opening will release a drop of liquid at a specific rate, and the drops will usually be within sight of one another. If you come to a fork in a road, you only have to look down each road to see the drops and know which way the spy has gone.

New high-tech electronic devices have reduced the use of this type of vehicle tracking. A small electronic device is attached to the spy's vehicle. This device gives off an electronic signal that is picked up by a tracking receiver. The tracking receiver can tell whether the vehicle is moving left, right, straight, or standing still. Electronic signals can even be picked up by satellites to determine the exact location of the vehicle.

"Goldilocks Calling Papa Bear"

Making Contact and Sending Secret Messages

When secret agents go under cover, they still need to communicate with others. Secret agents always have a contact to whom they pass information or from whom they get information. Often, spy operations are run by a **controller**, an agent assigned to supervise the operation.

Spies may be sent on a mission without knowing their contact. They may only know their contact by a code name. Scientific techniques are used in order to make sure that a spy meets with the true contact. The spy must also be sure that any messages sent to the contact will not be intercepted by enemy agents. Try the activities in this chapter to learn how spies use science to make contact and send secret messages.

Project 1

Torn Dollars

You are a secret agent and are supposed to meet your contact, who is someone you've never met before. How will you know that the person you meet is the right person and not an enemy agent? Try the following activity to learn one way spies make contact.

MATERIALS

scissors
ruler
sheet of green construction paper
3 helpers

1 Cut the sheet of paper into three 3-by-6-inch (7.5-by-15-cm) rectangles.

2 Give one piece of paper to each helper. Have your helpers tear their pieces of paper in half once, trying to make the three tears identical.

3 Leave the room.

4 Have the helpers select one person to be your contact. The contact should place half of his torn paper in the center of the room and the other half in his pocket.

5 The other helpers should place half of their torn paper in their pockets and throw the other halves away.

6 Reenter the room, and pick up the piece of paper in the center of the room. Try to match that half to those of your helpers. Can you find the matching half and your contact?

MORE FUN STUFF TO DO

Repeat the activity, but decorate the pieces of paper to look like dollar bills. Does this make it easier to match the two halves of the paper?

Paper is made of wood fibers that have been pressed together. The fibers are randomly arranged in the paper and can be of various lengths. When you tear paper, the fibers come apart. Since no two pieces of paper have fibers of the same length and arrangement, all paper tears differently. Even if you tried, you could not make identical tears in two pieces of paper.

Spies still use this method to ensure that the person they are meeting is who they are supposed to be. A spy will tear a fake dollar bill in half and give half to his controller, who then passes that half to the proper contact. The spy then matches his half to the contact's half to verify that the contact is the right person.

Project 2: Passive Contacts

Secret agents do not actually have to meet their contacts in person. There are many other ways to transfer information. Try the following activity to investigate one way.

MATERIALS

pencil   can opener

sheet of paper   helper

empty soda can

PROCEDURE

1. With your helper, choose a contact location. For example, you might choose a tree in your yard. Tell the helper to check the location daily.

2 The next day, write a secret message on the sheet of paper.

3 Fold the message and place it in the soda can.

4 Place the can in the designated location for your helper to pick up.

5 After your helper picks up the can, she should use the can opener to open the can and retrieve the message.

MORE FUN STUFF TO DO

Have your helper send a message back to you, using a different soda can. What are the problems with this type of message system?

EXPLANATION

This type of system for sending messages is called **passive contact.** In passive contact, two spies, or a spy and a contact, may never actually meet face-to-face to exchange information. One spy leaves information in a specific location for another spy or contact to pick up. This is called an **information drop.** Passive contact may also be used to indicate that an information drop is about to take place.

This type of system works well if one spy is being tailed. By making passive contact, the spy does not reveal her contacts to enemy agents. The enemy agent may only see someone going to a tree and picking up a soda can. The agent will not know who put the can there.

Common objects, like soda cans, are useful for sending messages, because no one notices them. Also, your contact could go under cover as a garbage collector, so that it would not be unusual for her to be seen picking up objects like empty soda cans. However, the risk of using common objects to send messages is that a message may sit in the container for days before the contact notices it, or the container could be thrown away before the contact gets to it.

John Walker was a spy for the former Soviet Union. For many years he delivered stolen U.S. Navy secrets to agents of the KGB (Komitet gosudarstvennoy bezopasnosti), the Soviet intelligence agency, working in Maryland. They often used passive contact to signal each other when an information drop was to be made.

The KGB agents would place an empty 7-Up can upright on the roadside at an agreed-upon spot. This signaled John Walker that his KGB contact was in the area and ready to make an exchange. The next move was up to him. Five miles (8 km) away, he would put a 7-Up can upright on the roadside to signal that he was ready. Then he would continue to the information drop location, where he would leave his bundle of classified documents near a telephone pole. At the same time that Walker was dropping off his package, the KGB was dropping off a package of cash for him at a spot a few miles (km) away. This activity continued for twenty years, until Walker was caught by the FBI and charged with espionage.

Rubber Bands

Project 3

You need to get secret information to a contact. You have set up a meeting at a café on the other side of town. When you arrive, your contact is sitting at a booth near the back of the café. You take a booth nearby and wait. Suddenly someone else enters the café. Have either of you been followed? You can't risk direct contact, and you haven't planned a passive contact. What do you do? Try the following activity to discover one way.

rubber band, at least ½ inch (1.25 cm) wide
book
ballpoint pen

1. Stretch the rubber band as much as possible and wrap it around the book.

2. Use the pen to write a message on the rubber band, such as "Matthew is a double agent. Beware."

3. Take the rubber band off the book. Observe the message when the rubber band is slack.

4. Send your message to your contact by shooting the rubber band at a wall across the room. Place the index finger of one hand inside the rubber band. Using the other hand to aim the rubber band at the wall, stretch and release the rubber band.

CAUTION: Never aim a rubber band at a person.

When you stretch the rubber band, the molecules that make up the rubber band are stretched apart. **Molecules** are particles made up of two or more bonded **atoms** (the smallest particles of matter). By writing on the stretched rubber band, you place the ink on the molecules in their stretched form. When the band is relaxed, the molecules move back closer together and the writing looks like a bunch of lines, rather than specific words. The message is hidden. After receiving the rubber band, your contact will need to stretch it again in order to read the secret message.

The rubber band travels across the room because of elastic energy. **Elastic energy** is the energy stored in a material when its shape is changed. When you stretch the rubber band between your fingers, you change the shape of the rubber band. The stretched rubber band contains stored elastic energy. Energy is never used up; it is just converted, or changed, from one form to another. When you release the rubber band, the elastic energy is converted to **kinetic energy,** the energy of movement. Kinetic energy causes the rubber band to fly across the room to the wall near your contact.

Small Secrets

Project 4

Messages are easier to hide if they are small. Try the following activity to see how to send a small message.

MATERIALS

postage stamp   pencil sharpener
envelope   sheet of paper
pencil

NOTE: Get an adult's permission before using the stamp.

1 Without licking the back of the stamp, lay it on the top right corner of the envelope.

2 Use the pencil to lightly outline the stamp. Remove the stamp. There should be a small rectangle drawn on the envelope the same size as the stamp.

3 Sharpen the pencil, and write a message inside the rectangle, writing as small as possible.

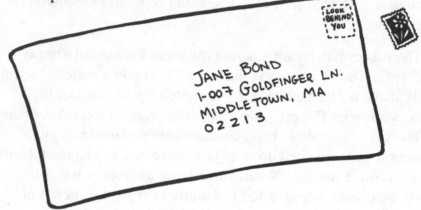

4 After you have written the message, lick the stamp and stick it on the envelope so that it fits inside the rectangle and covers the message.

5 Use the paper to write a letter to yourself. You can write anything you wish.

6 Place the paper in the envelope, seal it, and address the envelope to yourself. Place the stamped letter in the mailbox, and wait for it to be delivered back to you. Your secret message has been sent.

 MORE FUN STUFF TO DO

Remove the stamp, using the procedure in Chapter 2, Project 4, "Opening Letters." Can you read your message?

In this activity, you used miniature writing to send a secret message. You wrote as small as possible to fit your message under a postage stamp. Spies have used miniature writing for years as a method for sending secret messages.

Today, rather than handwrite the message, a secret agent makes a microcopy of the information. A **microcopy** is a photographic copy of either printed material or pictures in a very reduced size. A spy takes a photograph of a message or other information with a special camera. The camera reduces the size of the negative and places it on special film called **microfilm.** The microfilm, or miniature negative, can be placed under a stamp or hidden in some other secret location. Microcopy allows a great deal of information to be passed on by greatly reducing the size of the printing.

You may have seen microcopy in action at the library. Most libraries have years' worth of newspaper and magazine articles stored on something called microfiche. **Microfiche** are sheets of microfilm containing rows of pages of printed material that has been microcopied. A special viewer magnifies the pages and allows you to read the material.

During the Civil War, agents working for the Confederate army made miniature messages by taking pictures of the messages with special lenses on their cameras. They hid the miniature negatives inside metal buttons sewed onto their coats. The agents could then carry valuable information across enemy lines without being discovered. This technique eventually led to microcopy, the method today's spies use to make and send miniature messages.

SPY SCIENCE IN ACTION

Lemony Message

Enemy agents can't read a secret message if it's invisible.
There are several easy ways to make invisible messages.
Try the following activity to learn how to make an invisible
message using lemon juice.

MATERIALS

¼ cup (65 ml) lemon juice

small jar

cotton swab, such as a Q-Tips swab

sheet of white paper

lamp with lightbulb

PROCEDURE

1   Put the lemon juice in the jar.

2   Dip the cotton swab
    into the lemon juice, and
    write a message, such as
    "Secret meeting tonight at
    8:00," on the sheet of
    paper.

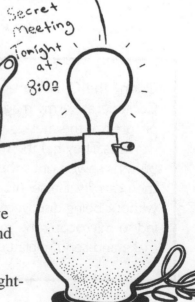

3   Allow the message
    to dry. You should
    not be able to see the
    message after it has dried.

4   When the message is dry, remove
    the lamp shade from the lamp and
    turn the lamp on.

5   Hold the message close to the light-
    bulb. What happens?

MORE FUN STUFF TO DO

1. Try other liquids for this activity, such as orange juice or vinegar. Do they also work?

2. Try using this technique to send a secret message to a friend. Put the message on a blank sheet of paper, or on a blank part of another paper that has other writing on it, such as a letter to your friend.

EXPLANATION

Lemon juice is very light colored and is difficult to see after it has dried. However, when you hold the paper close to the light-bulb, the heat from the bulb turns the lemon juice brown, and the hidden message appears. Fruit juices, including lemon juice and many other liquids, such as milk and soda, contain carbon atoms. In lemon juice, these carbon atoms are bonded to other atoms to form carbon-containing molecules.

These carbon-containing molecules have almost no color when dissolved in liquid. When these liquids are heated, however, a chemical reaction occurs. The carbon-containing molecules break apart and produce, among other substances, the element carbon. An **element** is a substance that cannot be further broken down chemically. **Carbon** is an element made up of carbon atoms that is found in all living matter. Carbon is black or brown in color, which is why the lemon juice turns brown when heated. Carbon also appears when you cook a piece of toast, which is why toast turns dark brown or black when burned.

Milky Beginning

Project
6

Believe it or not, you can write an invisible message using milk. Try another method for invisible writing.

¼ cup (65 ml) whole (4%)
  homogenized milk

small jar

cotton swab, such as a Q-Tips swab

sheet of white paper

pencil

sandpaper

1 Put the milk in the jar.

2 Dip the cotton swab into the milk, and write a message, such as "Message received, meeting confirmed," on the sheet of paper.

3 Allow the message to dry completely. This may take as long as an hour. Do not try to blot the message. You should not be able to see the message after it has dried.

4 When the message is completely dry, hold the pencil lead over the message area of the paper. Use the sandpaper to scrape the lead so that a black powder covers the message.

5 Gently rub the powder over the message area of the paper with your finger. What happens?

MORE FUN STUFF TO DO

1. Try other kinds of milk, such as 1% or 2%. Do they work as well as whole milk?

2. Try using this technique to send a secret message to a friend. Put the message on a blank sheet of paper, or on a blank area of another paper that has other writing on it, such as a letter to your friend.

EXPLANATION

Milk contains many chemicals mixed in water. One of these chemicals is **fat,** a food nutrient. The milk used in the activity is **homogenized,** which means that the fat has been made very fine and spread evenly throughout the milk. The fat is nearly invisible when it dries on white paper.

When you scrape the pencil lead, however, the fat becomes visible. Pencil lead is made of **graphite,** which is a form of the element carbon. The graphite scrapings stick to the fat in the dried milk but not to the rest of the paper, allowing the hidden message to appear. Because there is less fat in 1% and 2% milk than in whole milk, the experiment does not work as well with those kinds of milk.

Starchy Starts

Project 7

Some invisible writing is more complicated to do than others. Try the following investigation, using another chemical reaction.

several sheets of newspaper

2 sheets of plain white paper

scissors

spray starch

2 teaspoons (10 ml) tincture of iodine solution

1 cup (250 ml) water

empty spray bottle

CAUTION: Avoid getting tincture of iodine on your hands. It can stain.

P R O C E D U R E

1 Cover your work area with newspaper.

2 Using one sheet of white paper, cut out letters to spell a secret message, such as "Meet me after school."

3 Place the second sheet of white paper on the newspaper. Lay the letters for the message, in proper order, on the second sheet of paper.

4 Spray the sheet of paper and the letters with the spray starch.

5 Remove the letters and allow the sheet of paper to dry. This should take about 15 minutes, depending on the amount of spray starch you used. The message should be invisible.

6 Combine the tincture of iodine and the water together in the spray bottle. Shake the bottle to mix the solution.

7 Spray the paper with the water-and-iodine solution. What happens?

Try making a shape, such as a snowflake, placing it on the paper and spraying it with the spray starch as before. You can use this method to send pictures as well as written messages.

EXPLANATION

Starch is made up of sugar molecules linked together in a long chain. Iodine is an element made up of iodine molecules. When the iodine solution hits the starch-covered part of the paper, a chemical reaction occurs. The sugar molecules of starch and the iodine molecules combine to form complex starch-iodine molecules that are purple in color. Neither sugar by itself nor sugar molecules combined in any other way will react with iodine to produce this color.

The part of the paper underneath the letters was protected from the spray starch, so it remains white. The rest of the paper, where the starch was sprayed, turns a light purple due to the reaction of the starch with the iodine spray. The message will be visible as white letters on a purple background.

Egg-citing Messages

Project 8

There are many ways that a spy can send a secret message to a contact. Secret messages can even be sent in your lunch. Try the following activity to learn how.

egg   2 cups (500 ml) vinegar
saucepan   watch or clock
tap water   scouring powder
white wax crayon   soft brush
glass jar   adult helper

P R O C E D U R E

NOTE: This activity requires adult help.

1   Have your adult helper hard-boil the egg, using the saucepan and tap water.

2   Allow the egg to cool, then use the crayon to write a secret message on it, such as "Meet me at 1:00. Important."

3   Place the egg in the jar and add enough of the vinegar to cover the egg. Tiny bubbles should form on the egg. Allow the jar to sit undisturbed for 2 hours.

4   After 2 hours, pour the vinegar out of the jar, without pouring out the egg.

5   Add the remaining vinegar, again being sure to cover the egg. Allow the jar to sit undisturbed for 4 hours.

6   After 4 hours, rinse the egg under running water. While holding the egg under the water, gently remove the wax from the egg with the scouring powder and soft brush. Your message should stand out in raised letters.

E X P L A N A T I O N

The process you have experimented with is called **etching,** using an acid to make a drawing or design on another material. Vinegar is an **acid** (sour substance that reacts with a base to form salt and turns litmus red). Eggshells are made mainly of

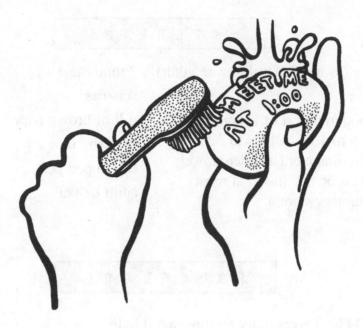

minerals, naturally occurring, nonliving substances. When you add vinegar to the egg in the jar, a chemical reaction occurs. The acid in the vinegar reacts with a mineral called calcium carbonate in the eggshell, causing the calcium carbonate to dissolve.

However, where you have written your message, the wax protects the eggshell, keeping the vinegar from reacting with the calcium carbonate. The vinegar dissolves the rest of the eggshell, allowing the secret message to stand out and become visible when the wax is removed.

But be careful with your message egg. An eggshell is only about $\frac{1}{10}$ inch (0.25 cm) thick. When the vinegar dissolves away half of that thickness, the eggshell becomes *very* fragile.

Scytale

One of the oldest known tools for communicating secret messages is the scytale. Try the next activity to make your own.

saw (to be used only by an adult)
ruler
wooden dowel or broomstick,
   ¾ to 1 inch (1.88 to 2.5 cm)
   in diameter (wooden dowel
   can be purchased at most
   lumber stores)

2 thumbtacks
scissors
roll of brown paper
masking tape
felt-tipped pen
adult helper

PROCEDURE

NOTE: This activity requires adult help.

1 Have the adult helper saw two 12-inch (30-cm) -long pieces from the dowel.

2 Stick a tack partway into each dowel, about ½ inch (1.25 cm) from the end.

3 Give the second dowel to your helper.

4 Cut the brown paper into a strip that is ¼ to ½ inch (0.63 to 1.25 cm) wide and 24 inches (60 cm) long.

5 Remove the tack from the first dowel.

6 Stick the tack through one end of the paper strip. Reinsert the tack and the strip in the hole in the dowel.

7 Wrap the paper strip around the dowel in a tight spiral so that the top edge of each turn just touches the bottom edge of the previous turn. Tape the end of the strip to the dowel.

8 Using a secret message, such as "You are being followed," write one letter of the message in each section of paper along the dowel, as shown. For a word space, leave the section blank.

9 Remove the tape from the end of the strip, unwrap the strip, and remove the tack. Give the strip to your helper.

10 Have the helper make the secret message readable by using the second dowel and tack, and repeating steps 6 and 7.

 MORE FUN STUFF TO DO

Try to make the message readable, using a dowel that is either larger or smaller than the one you used to write it. What happens?

EXPLANATION

The dowel-and-tack device you and your helper used is an ancient tool called the **scytale.** The message on the paper strip looks like a jumble of letters when your helper receives it. However, when your helper tacks the strip to the matching dowel and rewraps it in a tight spiral, the letters of the message line up neatly next to one another just as they were written.

For the scytale to work, the dowels of the person who sends the message and the dowels of the person who receives it must have the same circumference. The circumference is the distance that the paper took when it made one trip around the dowel. The distance between the letters on the paper equals the circumference of the dowel.

The circumference of any circle is found by the formula $C = \pi d$, where $\pi = 3.14$ and d equals the diameter. If the dowel you use has a diameter of ½ inch (1.25 cm), then the circumference of the dowel and the distance between the letters in your message would be 1.57 inches (3.93 cm). Your helper can read the message using another dowel with a ½-inch (1.25-cm) diameter. But if your helper uses a dowel of a different size to try to read it—for example, a dowel with a ¾-inch (1.88-cm) diameter—the result will be different. The letters will be 2.36 inches (5.9 cm) apart, they will not line up, and the message will not be readable.

Sparta was a great military city in Greece in 400 B.C. In order to exchange military information, Spartan generals used twin scytales and strips of parchment. Even if a message were intercepted, only the person who had a matching scytale could rewind the parchment and restore the original order of letters. The generals often used scytales of several different diameters and a code at the start of the parchment that told the reader which scytale to use.

Project 10 — Page Grills

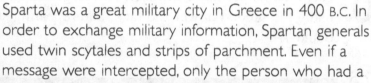

As with scytales, sending messages with page grills only works if the writer and the reader have the same devices. Try the following activity to see how page grills work.

MATERIALS

scissors

2 pieces of lightweight cardboard

sheet of graph paper, 4 or 5 squares to the inch

rubber cement

pencil

matte knife (to be used only by an adult)

2 paper clips

sheet of white paper

adult helper

NOTE: This activity requires adult help.

1   Use the scissors to cut each piece of cardboard to the same size as the sheet of graph paper.

2   Brush rubber cement on the back of the sheet of graph paper, and glue it to one piece of cardboard.

3   Lightly outline a large square on the graph paper that is 15 by 15 squares.

4   Mark an X in 25 of the squares inside the penciled area. Choose the squares at random; it does not matter which squares you choose.

5   Have an adult use the matte knife to carefully cut out all the squares marked with an X. You now have a page grill.

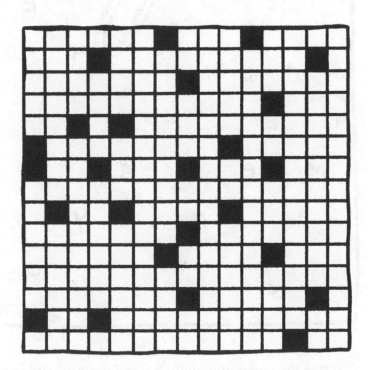

6   Lay the page grill over the second piece of cardboard, and hold them together with a paper clip.

7 Trace the outside edges of the cutout squares onto the second piece of cardboard. Remove the paper clip, and separate the grill and cardboard.

8 Have the adult cut out the squares in the second piece of cardboard. You now have two grills with identical cutout squares. Keep one and give the other to your helper.

9 Place the sheet of white paper behind your grill, and use a paper clip to hold it in place. Write the letters of a message, such as "I need help! Meet me at my house," through the cutout squares of the grill onto the white paper. Write the letters the same way you read: from left to right, and in rows from top to bottom.

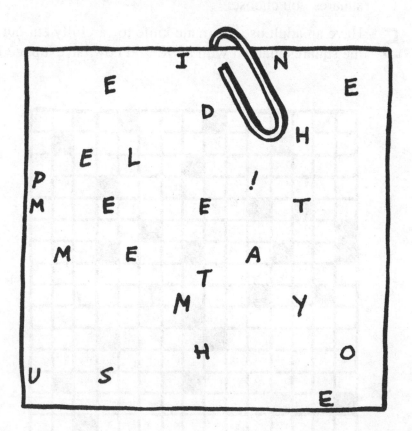

10 Remove the paper clip, and separate the grill and paper. Write other randomly chosen letters on the paper among the ones included in the message. Place them above, below, to the sides, and in between the letters of the message so that the message cannot be read.

11 Pass the paper to your helper. Have your helper read the message by laying the message sheet behind her copy of the grill and holding them together with a paper clip.

E X P L A N A T I O N

The cutouts in your page grill determine the order in which you write the letters. Without the matching grill, it is impossible to read the secret message. The message is hidden among the extra letters you added to the page. However, with the grill in place, your helper can read the letters that appear through the cutouts in the grill. Only the person who has a matching page grill can read the message.

Even the sculptures at the Central Intelligence Agency (CIA) headquarters in McLean, Virginia, hold secret messages. At the entrance to their new building is a copper sculpture, designed by the **architect** (building designer) Jim Sanborn. The sculpture stands more than 6 feet (2 m) high and looks like a scroll. On the scroll are letters that seem to make no sense. However, to the right of the sculpture is a plate with carved letters that represent a table, similar to a page grill, that can be used to translate the two thousand–word message.

The message actually describes the information-gathering role of the CIA. When the artwork was first put on display in November 1990, Sanborn gave the director of the CIA a translated copy of the text, just in case the CIA couldn't figure it out. (A picture of the sculpture, call Kryptos, is located on the CIA's home page. See Chapter 2, Project 2, "Internet Intrigue," to learn how to access this site.)

5 Cipher Secrets

Making (and Breaking) Codes

Secret agents know that one of the best ways to send a secret message is to use a code. A **code,** also called a **cipher**, is a method of changing words and sentences in order to hide their meanings. A code is often a system of symbols in which each symbol represents something else, usually a letter or a word. The symbols of a code can be letters, numbers, words, or even pictures.

When you change a message into a code, you **encode** or **encipher** it. When you translate an encoded message back into its regular form, you **decode** or **decipher** it. A message written in code or cipher is called a **cryptogram. Cryptology** is the study of making and breaking codes.

By now, you shouldn't be surprised to learn that science helps spies make and break codes. Try the following activities to learn some spy cipher secrets.

Project 1 Words in the Way

There are many ways to use codes to hide secret messages A secret message can be hidden in an ordinary letter. Try the following activity to see how.

MATERIALS

pencil
sheet of paper

PROCEDURE

Read the letter below. In it is a message.

Jack,

Thomas says hello. He now lives out in the country, but he does not enjoy it. Heard from Sarah. Recently she changed schools, but she seems to be doing fine. Initially, my school year was slow. Teachers were nice, and so were the other students. About two weeks ago, I turned in my term paper and things got better. My belief is that it is the best paper I have ever written and I hope to get a good grade. Hal, my English teacher, is an excellent teacher and I enjoy his class. In general I do better in great classes. I better end now. My neighbor is at the door and he wants me to mow his lawn. Until later.

J.

2 To decode the hidden message, use the pencil and paper to write down the third letter in the first word and then the third letter after every punctuation mark.

3 Divide the letters into words to read the secret message.

MORE FUN STUFF TO DO

Use this method of secret writing to send a message to a friend. Begin by writing something easy, such as "Meet me after school." Try different ways of hiding the message. Use the first or second letter after every punctuation mark, rather than the third, to indicate the letters that make up your message, or use the first and last letters of each sentence.

The punctuation marks in the letter are the comma (,) and the period (.). If you write down the third letter after each punctuation mark, you get the message "Contact is a double agent."

The code used in this activity tells you that every third letter after a punctuation mark is important. The person receiving the message must know the code in order to read the secret message. This type of code writing is difficult because you must place words with specific letters at specific places in each sentence to spell out your message. It can be very hard to spell out the message and make the letter sound natural at the same time.

However, this is a difficult code to break. If the letter is written well, an enemy agent may not realize it contains a secret message. Even if the agent realizes there is a hidden message, if he doesn't know the code, it may be impossible to figure out which words spell out the message.

SPY SCIENCE IN ACTION

During the seventeenth century in England, Oliver Cromwell, a religious and political leader, overthrew the English king, Charles I, and ruled the country for a brief time. During Cromwell's rule, many people remained loyal to the king. They were called Royalists and were imprisoned if caught. One of those caught was Sir John Trevenion.

Like other Royalists before him, Sir John would probably have been put to death for **treason** (attempting to betray or overthrow the government). However, several days before his execution, he received a simple letter. In the letter was a hidden message written with the code you just investigated. The secret message read, "Panel at east end of chapel slides."

Trevenion requested a private hour inside the prison chapel. But instead of spending the entire time in prayer, he escaped out the false panel in the chapel that he had learned about in the letter.

Quick Code

Suppose you need to send a secret message in code but you only have a few minutes. You need a fast, easy method. Try the next activity to learn a simple code to send secret messages.

MATERIALS

pencil

sheet of paper

PROCEDURE

1 Write the message "MEETING CALLED OFF. I'M BEING FOLLOWED." on the paper.

2 That message in code would read, "GNITEEM DELLAC FFO. M'I GNIEB DEWOLLOF." Can you figure out the code?

MORE FUN STUFF TO DO

Try to decode the phrase "PLEH DEEN I." What's different about this code? Write secret messages to your friends, using this code and the one from the original activity.

In the original activity, the message is encoded by writing each word backwards. In the More Fun Stuff to Do section, the entire sentence is written backward. This sentence translates to "I NEED HELP."

These codes are easy to write, but also easy to break. Because the encoded sentences are unreadable, an enemy agent will know right away that they are in code. Like you, a smart agent will be able to quickly break the code by reversing the words or letters.

The artist and scientist Leonardo da Vinci used a variation of this kind of code writing. He wrote backward, reversing each letter and writing from right to left across the page. He used this type of writing for many of his scientific manuscripts so that others couldn't steal his experiments. For backward writing to be read, it must be held up to a mirror. In the mirror the writing is reversed and can be read. Try backward writing and see if you can do it. You should be able to be read it when you hold it in front of a mirror.

Caesar Cipher

Historians believe that Julius Caesar, leader of the Roman Empire in 50 B.C., used a secret code made up of two alphabets. Try the following activity to learn one of the oldest secret codes.

MATERIALS

2 sheets of ruled paper
pencil

PROCEDURE

1 On one sheet of paper, write out the alphabet from *a* to *z*, leaving two blank lines beneath each row of letters.

2 Write the alphabet again underneath the first alphabet, only this time begin by placing the letter *a* under the letter *d* of the first alphabet so that the whole alphabet shifts to the right by three letters. Continue the alphabet from *a* to *z*. When you reach the letter *z* of the first alphabet (when you write the letter *w*), go back to the letter *a* in the first alphabet and finish the second alphabet.

3 On the second sheet of paper, decode the message "Ybtxob, Zxbpxo. Yorqrp fp x qoxfqlo!" Find each letter of the message on the second alphabet and replace it with the letter from the first alphabet. For example, replace the letter *x* with the letter *a*, the letter *y* with the letter *b*, and so on.

 MORE FUN STUFF TO DO

Use this method to write secret messages to your friends. Can they decode your messages? Try moving the second alphabet more or fewer letters to the right to change the code.

EXPLANATION

The message from the original activity reads, "Beware, Caesar. Brutus is a traitor!" Julius Caesar never actually received that encoded message. If he had, he might have learned the truth about his friend Brutus, who later turned on Caesar.

This code, called **Julius Caesar cipher,** uses letters to represent other letters by writing one alphabet below another and shifting the second alphabet one or more letters to the right. Historians believe that Julius Caesar used this simple code in writing his correspondence. This code is called Julius Caesar cipher, regardless of how many letters the lower alphabet is shifted. In this activity, the letters in the second alphabet are shifted three letters to the right. Although this is an easy code to write, it is also an easy code to break, as you will see in the next activity.

Most experts consider Johannes Trithemius, Abbot of Spanheim in Germany, to be the father of modern **cryptography,** the art of writing in code or cipher. In 1510, Trithemius wrote *Polygraphia,* the first printed work on cryptology.

Trithemius also created the first **cipher table,** a square table in which the alphabet is written 26 times. Each alphabet fills one row of the table, and each successive alphabet is shifted one more letter to the left. For example, the first letter of the second alphabet is *B;* the first letter of the third is *C,* and so on. Each alphabet in turn is used to encipher each letter of a secret message. The first letter of the message is enciphered with the first alphabet, the second letter with the second alphabet, and so on. Using this method, the word *secret* becomes *Sfeuiy.* This method of secret writing was used extensively in the 1500s.

SPY SCIENCE IN ACTION

Cracking the Code

Spies often intercept messages sent by enemy agents. An encoded message will not help the spy unless she can figure out how to decode it. Try the following activity to learn one way to break a secret code.

Julius Caesar cipher (see Chapter 5, Project 3, "Caesar Cipher")
pencil
2 sheets of ruled paper
helper

1 Have your helper write you a simple message of 10 to 15 words, using the Julius Caesar cipher, the pencil, and one sheet of paper. When she makes the cipher, she should move the second alphabet to the right either more or fewer letters than the three letters used in the Caesar cipher activity.

2 When you receive the message, try to break the code. Begin by writing out the alphabet on the second sheet of paper, leaving two blank lines beneath each row of letters.

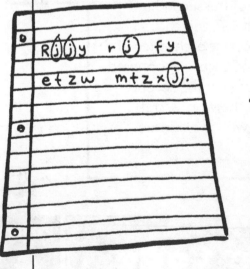

3 Count the number of times each letter is used in the message. Circle the letter that is used most often.

4 On your alphabet sheet, find the letter most often used in the message. Write the letter *e* under the letter.

5 Write the rest of the alphabet under the first alphabet.

6 Decode the secret message on the first sheet of paper, using your alphabet code.

7 If you are unable to decode the message, repeat the activity, trying the letter *t* instead of *e* to stand for the most often used letter. If you are still not successful, continue to repeat the activity, trying the letter *a*, then *i*, *s*, *o*, and *n*, until you find the letter that cracks the code.

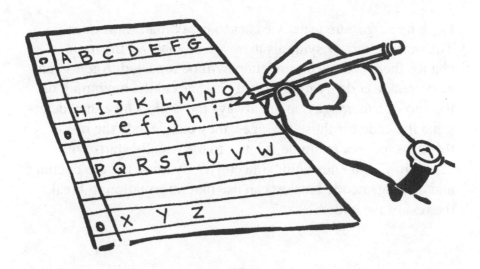

MORE FUN STUFF TO DO

The game of hangman helps sharpen your code-breaking skills. To play, have your helper think of a word and then make a series of short blanks for every letter in that word. Begin the game by asking if a certain letter is in the word. If it is, your helper should write that letter in the appropriate blank(s). If it isn't, she gets to draw a part of a body to be hanged, beginning with the head, then the body, arms, and legs. After you have chosen several correct letters, try to guess the word your helper chose. For advanced hangman, use phrases instead of words.

EXPLANATION

The most commonly used letter in the English language is the letter *e*. After that come the letters *t, a, i, s, o,* and *n*. Other commonly used letters are *l, d, u,* and *g*. The letters *b, c, h, m, p, v, w, j, f, r, x, k, q,* and *y* are used less often. Do you know what letter is used the least often? The letter *z*. The letter *e* is found over fifty times more often than the letter *z!*

Long messages are usually easier to break than short ones. The more letters or symbols there are to analyze, the more chance there is that certain letters will be repeated. Agents can also break a code by figuring out passages at the beginning or the end of a message that are always the same. Once they determine the code for those passages, they can decode the rest of the message. For example, a letter to me usually starts with "Dear Jim" and ends with "Sincerely." By knowing the opening and closing, a code breaker can use that information to break the rest of the code.

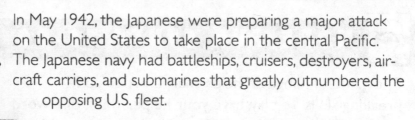

SPY SCIENCE IN ACTION

In May 1942, the Japanese were preparing a major attack on the United States to take place in the central Pacific. The Japanese navy had battleships, cruisers, destroyers, aircraft carriers, and submarines that greatly outnumbered the opposing U.S. fleet.

The Americans had broken the Japanese code and knew the major attack was coming, but they did not know exactly where. Japanese communication named the target by the letters AF. There were many targets in the central Pacific that could be attacked, such as Oahu in the Hawaiian Islands or the Midway islands. No one was sure.

To solve the mystery, two naval intelligence officers, Commander Joseph Rochefort and E.T. Layton, thought of a brilliant plan. They had the Americans at the Midway base radio naval headquarters at Pearl Harbor to report that the water distillation plant at Midway had broken down. The message was deliberately sent uncoded.

Two days later, the Americans intercepted a coded Japanese message. The message reported that AF was short of drinking water because of a plant breakdown. The Americans then knew that AF was Midway. When the Japanese fleet came charging into the Midway islands for their major attack, the American fleet was ready and waiting.

Symbols

Not all codes involve using letters to hide a secret message. Try a simple code that uses symbols instead.

pencil
2 sheets of paper
helper

1   Write a simple message to send to a helper, such as "Meet me after school by the bike rack," on the first sheet of paper.

2   On the second sheet of paper, use the following code to encode the secret message, substituting each letter for its corresponding symbol. The symbol for each letter is the combination of lines, or the lines and the dot, that the letter occupies.

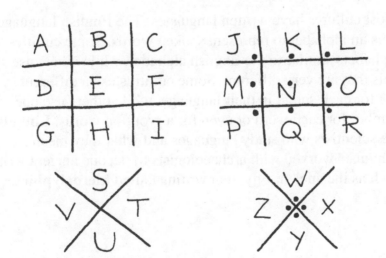

For example, the letter *a* is written as ⌋, the letter *b* is ⊔, the letter *o* is ⊡, the letter *u* is ⋀, and the letter w is ⋁. The word *code* would be written ⌊ ⊡ ⊐ ⊓.

3 Give the second sheet of paper to your helper. Ask your helper to use the code to decode the secret message, substituting each symbol for its corresponding letter.

MORE FUN STUFF TO DO

Try to invent your own code that uses symbols instead of letters. How well does it work? What problems occur when your helper tries to decode your message?

EXPLANATION

The code in this activity uses a system of symbols to represent letters. This type of code is easy to create, but to decode it, the reader must know the code the writer used. And if the reader knows the code but the code is too complicated, the reader still may not be able to decode it. Today, agents use computers to create and break codes. Because of advanced technology, a secret agent usually uses a code only one time, then uses a new code for the next message.

Most cultures have written languages. The English language uses an alphabet to represent spoken words. Some cultures use alphabets similar to the English alphabet, while others use symbols that are very different. Some cultures use a different symbol for each sound in their language, while others use one symbol for each word or even for a group of words. **Linguists** are scientists who study languages and what they mean. Linguists worked with archaeologists to decode ancient writing, such as the ancient Egyptian writing called **hieroglyphics.**

With all the complicated codes that the U.S Army, Navy, and Air Force had during World War II, the U.S Marines had a simple system that the Japanese could not break. The marines recruited Native American Navajos to man their combat radios. Navajos talked to Navajos, and the Japanese were not able to understand what they were saying. The Navajo language was an unbreakable code

Morse Code

There are ways to send encoded messages without writing them down. Try this activity to investigate a classic code.

MATERIALS

wire strippers or pliers (to be used only by an adult)

ruler

two 6-foot (2-m) pieces of insulated 22-gauge copper wire

one 12-inch (30-cm) piece of insulated 22-gauge copper wire

spring-type clothespin

6-volt dry-cell battery

4.5-volt lightbulb with bulb holder (available from most hardware stores)

screwdriver

pencil

sheet of paper

adult helper

NOTE: This activity requires adult help.

1 Have your adult helper use the wire strippers to remove ½ inch (1.25 cm) of insulation from the ends of all three wires and an additional 1 inch (2.5 cm) from one end of one of the long wires and one end of the short wire.

2 Using the wires with the additional insulation removed, wind the longer stripped ends around each tail end of the clothespin so that the wires touch when the clothespin is pinched.

3 Wrap the free end of the short clothespin wire around one of the battery terminals. Wrap the free end of the long clothespin wire around one screw terminal of the bulb holder, then tighten the screw with the screwdriver.

4 Use the other long wire to complete the circuit by wrapping one end around the other battery terminal and the other end around the other screw terminal of the bulb holder. When you pinch the clothespin, the bulb should light.

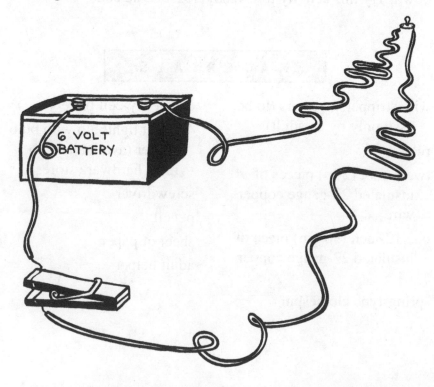

6 VOLT
BATTERY

5 Place the bulb as far away as the wire will allow. Send long and short flashes of light to your helper by pinching the clothespin together for 3 seconds for a long flash and 1 second for a short flash.

6 Have your helper record the light flashes by writing a dot for a short flash and a dash for a long flash.

MORE FUN STUFF TO DO

1. The code shown uses a series of dots and dashes to represent letters and numbers. Each letter in the alphabet and each number has its own symbol.

A ·_	J ·___	S ···	2 ··___
B _···	K _·_	T _	3 ···__
C _·_·	L ·_··	U ··_	4 ····_
D _··	M __	V ···_	5 ·····
E ·	N _·	W ·__	6 _····
F ··_·	O ___	X _··_	7 __···
G __·	P ·__·	Y _·__	8 ___··
H ····	Q __·_	Z __··	9 ____·
I ··	R ·_·	1 ·____	0 _____

Use this code to send a message to your helper. To indicate the end of one letter and the beginning of the next, flash for 5 seconds between letters. Flash for 7 seconds between words. Can you think of other ways to send this code? Try replacing the bulb with a bell or a buzzer as in Chapter 3, Project 8, "Alarm."

2. With an adult, use a flashlight to send a message outdoors on a dark night. Have your adult helper stand at least 50 yards (50 m) away. Cover the flashlight with your hand. Remove your hand for 1 second for a dot and 3 seconds for a dash. A 5-second flash marks the end of a letter; a 7-second flash, the end of a word.

E X P L A N A T I O N

The code you used in this activity is called **Morse code,** invented by Samuel Morse and first demonstrated in 1844. Morse also invented a machine called a **telegraph** to send messages in his code. In this activity, you built a model of Morse's telegraph.

Both Morse's telegraph and yours work because of electricity. For electricity to flow, electrons must travel from a source of energy—in this case, a battery—in an electric circuit. The circuit you made begins at one terminal of the battery, runs through the wires to the bulb, continues through the other wire, and ends at the other terminal of the battery.

In your telegraph, the circuit is not complete until the wires in the clothespin touch. When you pinch the clothespin, the wires touch, closing the circuit between the battery and the bulb. Electricity flows from the battery to the bulb and back to the battery, and the bulb lights. Your message is sent.

In Morse's telegraph, the operator presses a key to send signals. Pressing the key closes the electric circuit, allowing electricity to flow. The electricity activates either a clicker that clicks out long or short sounds that are recorded as dots or dashes, or an inker that actually prints out the dots and dashes. The dots and dashes are then decoded into words, using Morse code.

Glossary

acid   A substance that tastes sour, reacts with a base to form salt, and turns litmus red.

agent   A spy paid by a country's intelligence agency on a regular basis.

amplify   To make louder.

archaeologist   A scientist who learns about cultures from the past by studying their remains.

architect   A building designer.

artifacts   Objects that were used by people in the past.

atom   The smallest particle of matter.

behavioral scientist   A scientist who studies how other people act in certain situations.

bias   A judgment or opinion that may or may not match the facts.

bond   Join together by an attractive force.

browser   A computer software program, such as Netscape, Mosaic, or Telnet, used to look for information on the World Wide Web.

bug   A tiny recording device that can be hidden almost anywhere and can transmit conversations hundreds of yards (meters) away.

camouflage   To disguise, hide, or conceal something or someone so that the object or person is not easily seen.

carbon   An element made up of carbon atoms that is found in all living matter.

chemical reaction   A change in matter in which substances break apart to produce one or more new substances.

cipher   See **code**.

cipher table   A square table used to encode and decode secret messages, in which the alphabet is written in 26 rows, with each successive alphabet shifted one more letter to the left than the previous alphabet.

circumference   The distance around a circle. The circumference of any circle is found by the formula $C = \pi d$, where $\pi = 3.14$ and d is the diameter.

code   A method of changing written words in order to hide their meaning; also called cipher.

communicating   Exchanging information.

concave lens   A lens that is curved like the inside of a bowl.

condense   To change from a gas to a liquid.

contact   A person to whom a spy passes information or from whom the spy gets information.

controller   An agent assigned to supervise a spy operation.

convex lens   A lens that is curved like the outside of a ball.

cover   A disguise an agent uses to protect his or her identity and motives.

creative thinking   Showing imagination and inventiveness in solving a problem.

cryptogram   A message written in code or cipher.

cryptography   The art of writing in code or cipher.

cryptology   The study of making and breaking codes.

decipher   See **decode.**

decode   To translate an encoded message into ordinary language; also called decipher.

diameter   The length of a line passing through the center of a circle.

dissolve   To become liquid.

double agent   A person who spies for both sides.

elastic energy   The energy stored in a material when its shape is changed.

electric circuit   A complete circular path for electrons to travel from the energy source and back again.

electricity   A form of energy caused by the movement of electrons.

electron   A small, negatively charged particle.

element   A substance that cannot be broken down chemically.

encipher   See **encode.**

encode   To convert a message into code; also called encipher.

environmental scientist   A scientist who studies the interactions of living things in the world.

espionage   Spying.

etching   The process of using an acid to make a drawing or design on another material.

evaporate   To change from a liquid to a gas.

fat   A food nutrient.

fibers   Slender threadlike structures that give woody plants strength.

focus   The point where light rays meet or come together after passing through a lens; also the process of producing a clear image from refracted light.

geography   The branch of science that studies the surface of the earth.

graphite   A form of the element carbon.

hieroglyphics   Ancient Egyptian writing.

home page   The first page of a document on the World Wide Web; also called a Web site.

homogenize   To make very fine and spread out throughout.

hypothesis   An educated guess or theory.

inference   A conclusion.

infiltrate   To enter for secret purposes.

information drop   A passive contact by which information is left in a specific location for another agent to retrieve.

intelligence agency A government organization responsible for spies and spying.

intercept To receive a communication directed elsewhere.

Internet An *inter*connected *net*work that links computers all over the world through telephone lines.

invert To turn upside down.

Julius Caesar cipher A code believed to have been used by Julius Caesar that uses letters to represent other letters and that is made by writing one alphabet below another and shifting the lower alphabet one or more letters to the right.

kinetic energy The energy of movement.

legend A story that supports the cover a spy has chosen.

lens A curved piece of glass or other transparent substance that refracts light rays passing through it; also the part of the human eye that focuses refracted light at one point inside the eyeball.

lepidopterist A scientist who studies butterflies.

linguist A scientist who studies languages and what they mean.

magnified Enlarged.

microcopy A photographic copy of either printed material or pictures in a very reduced size.

microfiche Sheets of microfilm containing rows of pages of printed material that has been microcopied.

microfilm A miniature negative on which printed material or pictures are photographed at a greatly reduced size.

mineral A naturally occurring nonliving substance.

modem A device that converts the messages and commands on a computer screen into sendable electronic data.

mole A spy who works under cover for a long time in an enemy organization before beginning to collect secret information.

molecule A particle made up of two or more atoms bonded together.

Morse code A code invented in 1844 by Samuel Morse that uses a series of dots and dashes to communicate numbers and letters.

Northern Hemisphere The half of the earth between the equator and the north pole.

operation A spy mission.

parabolic microphone A microphone attached to a parabolic reflector to amplify sound.

parabolic reflector A bowl-like device that receives sounds and focuses them at one point.

passive contact An information exchange in which the spies do not meet.

periscope A device that uses mirrors to allow the viewer to see around corners and overhead.

photography   A process of producing images of objects on a special surface, such as film.

point retinal image   An image whose refracted light is in focus at one point inside the eyeball.

receiver   A device that turns the radio waves sent by a transmitter back into sound.

reflect   To bounce off a mirror or other object.

refract   To bend by use of a lens.

resonance   The process of reinforcing and amplifying a sound by reflecting its sound waves.

rotation   A turn.

scytale   A device used by the Spartans in ancient Greece that uses matching cylinders and strips of parchment paper to send secret messages.

server   A large computer that makes it possible for home computers to connect to the Internet.

spying   Observing closely and secretly.

steam   Tiny droplets of water that form as water vapor cools.

surface tension   The force of attraction between water particles that creates a thin skin on the surface of the water.

surveillance   A close watch kept over someone or something.

tail   To closely follow a person.

telegraph   A device that sends an encoded message to a distant location over electric wires.

transmit   To send.

transmitter   A device that sends messages from one place to another, often using radio waves.

treason   Attempting to betray or overthrow the government.

under cover   Using a cover.

vibrate   To move to and fro repeatedly.

water soluble   Able to dissolve in water.

water vapor   The gas form of water.

World Wide Web   A collection of documents on the Internet that contain information provided by government agencies, businesses, and educational institutions.

Index